FROM SOME FISSURE

THE REAL STORY BEHIND POPE PAUL VI

DAVID MARTIN

For information regarding permission, write to:
David Martin
5815 E. Olympic Bl
Los Angeles CA 90022
jmj4today@att.net

First edition June 2013
ISBN: 978-0-9896429-7-2

POPE PAUL VI

June 21, 1963 - August 6, 1978

DEDICATION

*This book is dedicated to Mary, Mother of the Church,
as She was so declared by Pope Paul VI on November 21, 1964*

CONTENTS

Papacy began: June 21, 1963
Papacy ended: August 6, 1978
Predecessor: John XXIII
Successor: John Paul I

Orders
Ordination: May 29, 1920 by Giacinto Gaggia
Consecration: December 12, 1954 by Eugène Tisserant
Created Cardinal: December 15, 1958 by John XXIII

Personal details
Birth name: Giovanni Battista Enrico Antonio Maria Montini
Born: September 26, 1897 Concesio, Italy
Died: August 6, 1978 (age 80), Italy

Motto
Cum Ipso in monte (With Him on the mount)
In nomine Domini (In the name of the Lord)

Coat of arms

Title as Saint: Venerable

PREFACE

Pope Paul VI was perhaps the most betrayed and misunderstood pope of history whose subjects took the law into their own hands and promulgated their designs in his name. He is generally seen as the spur of modernists and the scapegoat of dissatisfied Traditionalists, but according to His Holiness Benedict XVI, he should be seen as the saint of God whose "heroic virtues" warrant the official recognition of the Church.

On December 20, 2012, Benedict approved the plan to go forward with the process of Pope Paul's beatification, so this should serve as a spur for Catholics to follow through and look into the matter of his pontificate with a little more depth. It is commonly cited in Traditional circles that there is an enigma surrounding Paul VI, that there are certain mysteries or strange contradictions about him that simply don't add up. That is to say, they don't know the whole story about Paul VI.

Hence this Year of Faith is the acceptable time to read this story about Pope Paul and fill in the mysterious gaps, that it might revive our faith in the late pontiff and quell any suspicions that Benedict's initiative may have sparked.

When we speak of Paul VI, we speak of the conciliar pope who reigned during that turbulent period when the Church emerged from its past and moved forward with the times in a new-found quest to unite itself with the world. But he is also the pope who bewailed many of the new changes that diverted the Barque of Peter from its chartered course and landed it shipwreck onto secular coasts. The question we must ask ourselves is: who was really at the helm?

It is no secret that the pirates of reform hijacked the ship at Vatican II, the historic Council over which Paul VI presided. His role at Vatican II was of no small significance, since it made him the figure-head of the modernist reform which the Second Vatican Council had drafted under his jurisdiction.

However, Paul VI did not control Vatican II, as neither did the good bishops that attended. Rather, the Council was controlled by a clique of modernist innovators that derailed it in the opening session. Archbishop Lefebvre relates the scene: "From the very first days, the Council was besieged by the progressive forces. We experienced it, felt it…. It was then that a powerful, a very powerful organization showed its hand at the Council, set up by the cardinals from those countries bordering the Rhine." *(Open Letter to Confused Catholics, 1986)*

It was this Rhine coalition that set the Vatican Council on a new revolutionary path that was never planned by John XXIII and the original architects of Vatican II. The pope's plan was to simply restate and uphold the Church's Tradition in all its "undiluted purity," and to adopt a more effective means of projecting this orthodoxy to the world via the media. But his plan did not include the watering down of doctrine or the alteration of the Church's exterior lines. The original plan was rather strict and sterile in keeping with the Council of Trent, and unfortunately this didn't rest well with those purveyors of error that had already agreed amongst themselves that they were going "to block the first session by refusing to accept the tyrannical rules laid down by John XXIII." (Cardinal Tisserant, *Vatican II in the Dock,* 2003)

A key instigator of the pack was Fr. Edward Schillebeeckx of the Netherlands, a known heretic who denied the historicity of the Virgin Birth, the Resurrection, and the Eucharist (Transubstantiation), and who had drafted and disseminated a 480-page critique aimed at rallying the Rhine bishops to reject the original plan for Vatican II. The design of these progressivists was to revive the Reformation under the pretext of a renewal in order to justify it before the faithful. This plan was already in motion by the time Paul VI was elected.

Of the utmost importance to these reformers was the absolute need of having Pope Paul's signature on all the conciliar documents. This would be necessary to elicit the endorsement of the entire Council whereby the documents would appear to have the stamp of the Church's Magisterium, when in reality they would be the work of progressive innovators to destroy the Catholic Church.

To this end the documents were deliberately worded in ambiguous fashion, whereby liberal proposals were given a certain appearance of orthodoxy so as to appear blameless and worthy of support. Virtually everything in the Vatican II documents has this ambiguous, double meaning to it. For instance the term "religious communities" which normally would mean Catholic communities is often used in the documents to mean non-Catholic communities. The word "catholicity" which would normally mean our oneness with the Church of Rome is now used to mean oneness with the universal body of world churches, a theme that was central to the Council (ecumenism).

The Council's often repeated theme of "active participation by the faithful" was another ambiguous bombshell that had confused many a good bishop at the Council, the pope included. On the surface this would normally be taken to mean that Catholics should actively be involved with their religion by reading the lives of the saints, frequenting the sacraments, especially confession and communion, zealously attending the Latin High Mass, and sanctifying their souls in the fear of God. But what these draftsmen of perfidy really meant by this wording is that they should be busy-body activists engaging in the liturgical revolution against the priesthood by performing priestly functions on the altar as lectors and Eucharistic Ministers. This same activist theme was also their justification for inviting elements of culture and vernacular into the Mass as we see proposed in the documents (Sacrosanctum Concilium 36, 37).

Initially the pope in his trusting nature never realized he was being deceived; he never dreamed in his wildest nightmares that the devil had reached in and jinxed the Council documents. But soon after the "neo-Reformation" was established and rolling in left lane, the pope recognized what was happening and started pulling to the right which angered liberals to the point of resorting later to drastic measures to keep their plan going. But this they did in the name of Pope Paul VI, and because of this there is much prejudice and misinformation abounding today about the late pontiff, so much so, that it has caused some well-meaning Catholics to desert the Barque of Peter altogether.

It is enough to say that Paul VI was not the engineer of the modernist reform. With the buzz of activity surrounding him during those pivotal years, his true heart wasn't always evident before the Church. But as with any true pope, his favor rested with the remnant of the flock that holds to Tradition. Though he was open to dialogue with non-Catholics of all denominations, he did not think outside the Faith and did not encourage that his flock should do so. And whereas there was much in the way of non-Catholic thought and activity prevailing in the Church during his pontificate, he himself did not condone it, and in fact he went to considerable length to denounce it. Consider his words to the famous French Philosopher, Jean Guitton:

"What strikes me when I think of the Catholic world is that within Catholicism there seems sometimes to predominate a non-Catholic way of thinking, and it can happen that this non-Catholic thought within Catholicism will tomorrow become the stronger. But it will never represent the thought of the Church. It is necessary that a small flock subsist, no matter how small it might be." (Jean Guitton, *Paul VI Secret,* 1979)

Pope Paul's prophecy about this neo-Reformation of tomorrow is apparently what he meant shortly before the close of Vatican II when he told his friend, Guitton, "I am about to blow the seven trumpets of the Apocalypse." Pope Paul knew that the Church was about to embark upon the great apostasy foretold in the

Apocalypse, a spiritual blight that the Council will have launched. In his final speech at the end of Vatican II he warned of "profane and secular humanism" that had "defied the Council" and he stated that: "The religion of God made man has met the religion of man who makes himself God." (December 7, 1965) Herein he makes reference to the spiritual Armageddon that was already raging within the Church, from which would ensue this spiritual revolution of the end times. This Apocalyptic battle of the spirits was prophesied by John Paul II at the Eucharistic Congress in Philadelphia in 1976, when he said: "We are now facing the final confrontation between the Church and the anti-church, between the Gospel and the anti-gospel. It is a trial that the entire Church must take up."

Let it suffice to say, that Paul VI was not of the Reformationalist school. Above all, he was a very Marian pope, which is the truest mark of Catholicity. His expressed regret over the prevalence of non-Catholic thought in the Church should set the record straight concerning the true aversion he had for non-Catholic thinking. Hopefully, this will place his integrity into focus and provide a wholesome meditation for readers as they contemplate the papal mystery of Paul VI.

David Martin

"The Eucharistic Mystery stands at the heart and center of the liturgy, since it is the font of life by which we are cleansed and strengthened to live not for ourselves but for God."

-- Pope Paul VI, Mysterium Fidei, September 3, 1965

Coup d'etat at Vatican II

When the announcement was made on December 20, 2012, that Pope Benedict XVI had approved the cause for the beatification of Pope Paul VI, glaring eyebrows went up in the Traditionalist camp. After all, saints are usually martyr figures that are persecuted for their uncompromising fidelity to the Faith, and Paul VI is generally regarded as the compromising modernist who introduced destructive changes to the Mass that led the Church away from its own Tradition. But is this really true?

The common assumption is that the new order of change was Pope Paul's doing, since he was the visible head of the Church at a time when these innovative reforms were underway. But Paul VI was also the visible head of the Church at a time when artificial contraception was being adopted more and more by Catholic women, even with the blessing of liberal clergy, so did this mean that the escalating use of the "pill" was also his doing?

The truth is that Pope Paul VI did not initiate or design the New Mass. The authors of the New Liturgy only promulgated it in his name to give it credibility before the Church, but he himself was not the architect, nor did he pen the December 4, 1963, Concilium on the liturgy which bears his name. Whatever he did with respect to implementing a new Mass was done by way of permission, not by way of order, and with reservation at that.

The committee responsible for the changes in the Mass was already intact long before Pope Paul's election on June 21, 1963. The opening session of Vatican II was the historic coup d'etat that gave birth to the modernist reform so often attributed to Pope Paul VI. The game plan was to block the opening session by scrapping

John XXIII's outline for the Second Vatican Council, a plan that was kicked into play just hours after the Council commenced on October 11, 1962. This story of what happened at the Council is no secret, and has been told in great depth by the most qualified witnesses that were there. It is well worth recounting this incident to give us a better perspective of what took place in the immediate months prior to Pope Paul's election. (Fr. Ralph Wiltgen, *The Rhine Flows into the Tiber*)

At the center of this coup to [1] usurp the Council were Cardinals Alfrink, Frings, and Lienart of the "Rhine Alliance." A crucial vote was to be taken to determine the members of the conciliar drafting

commissions when Cardinal Lienart, a thirtieth degree Freemason, seized the microphone during a speech and demanded that the slate of 168 candidates be discarded and that a new slate of candidates be drawn up. His uncanny gesture was heeded by the Council and the election was postponed. Lienart's action deflected the course of the Council and made history, and was hailed a victory in the press. The date was October 13, 1962, the 45th Anniversary of Our Lady's last apparition at Fatima.

---

1   *We gather that Cardinal Tisserant, the key draftsman of the 1962 Moscow-Vatican Treaty who presided at the opening session, was at the center of this coup to usurp the Vatican Council. According to Jean Guitton, the famous French academic, Tisserant had showed him a painting of himself and six others, and told him, "This picture is historic, or rather, symbolic. It shows the meeting we had before the opening of the Council when we decided to block the first session by refusing to accept the tyrannical rules laid down by John XXIII." (Vatican II in the Dock, 2003)*

With the "election" that resumed, a number of radical theologians were then appointed to chair and advise the commissions, including Hans Kung, Rahner, de Lubac, Schillebeeckx and others whose writings had been blacklisted under Pius XII. The liberals now occupied nearly 60% of the seats, giving them the needed power to steer the Council in their direction.

Through deceitful promises and skillful use of the media, the Council approved their plan for a new Mass on December 7, 1962, known as the [2] "Constitution on the Sacred Liturgy," and this became the hub of the liturgical reform that was to set the Church on a new revolutionary course of change.

Hence by December 1962, the Vatican II Council was already out of control, so that by the time Paul VI was elected he was basically watching a locomotive go down the side of a mountain with no brakes. Even so, it had scarcely dawned on anyone that "the smoke of satan had entered the Church" since many of the conciliar proposals bore a serene exterior which seemed in the best interest of the Church. So the pope naturally did his best to try to work with the Council, believing that God was guiding its progress.

But by the end of the Council he was forced to acknowledge the contrary, stating that "profane and secular humanism has revealed itself in its terrible, anticlerical stature, and in one sense has defied the Council." (December 7, 1965) Three years later to the day he bewailed how the Church was questioning its own teachings, its

---

2   One of the key draftsmen of the Constitution was the radical theologian, Fr. Godfrey Diekmann, who along with Hans Kung and others had been blacklisted for his heretical views. Yet it was Godfrey who founded the ICEL for the purpose of implementing the Liturgical Constitution in the U.S and other English speaking countries. This only shows how the Constitution was drafted with the view that it should be implemented with all the novelty and inclusive language that we find in the Mass today. Today's creative liturgy grew out of the Constitution that he helped to draft. Bugnini, the founder of the Constitution, even stated during the implementative stage: "The greatest liberty was given to choose between the various formulas, to individual creativity." (Msgr. Annibale Bugnini, July 2, 1967)

own policies, its own Tradition. "The Church finds herself in an hour of anxiety, a disturbed period of self-criticism, or what would even better be called self-destruction. It is an interior revolution, acute and complicated, which nobody expected after the Council. It is almost as if the Church were attacking herself." (December 7, 1968 in his address to Lombardi Seminary)

It was on the ninth anniversary of his Coronation that Pope Paul VI lamented the outcome of Vatican II, when he stated to the world: "From some fissure the smoke of satan entered into the temple of God." (June 29, 1972) He pointed out how the work of God to enact holy reform had been hampered by "the devil" who was present "to suffocate the fruits of the Ecumenical Council," so that a new unexpected reform emerged. Five months later in his famous homily on the devil, he said, "One of the Church's greatest needs is to be defended against the evil we call the Devil." (General Audience, November 15, 1972)

Too bad the good pope wasn't quite on to this eight years earlier. On February 29, 1964, Pope Paul VI appointed Monsignor Annibale Bugnini to head the new Vatican II Consilium for the implementation of the Constitution on Sacred Liturgy, apparently not knowing that he had been dismissed earlier by John XXIII for sinister activity. Bugnini, of course, was the Masonic initiate who spearheaded the liturgical reform with the aid of his conciliar cronies, so it is good to diverge briefly to set the record straight about the origin of the New Mass, lest the wrong doing continue to be heaped upon Paul VI *(see Michael Davies, Liturgical Time Bombs in Vatican II)*.

The Bugnini Draft

If the engineers of the neo-Reformation were able to advance their plans and bring forth a new Mass for the Church in defiance of centuries of divine guidance, then it means they weren't being watched too carefully. While John XXIII and his men were busy at work preparing for the Second Vatican Council in the years preceding the Council, there lay hidden in the Vatican a secret cabal of liturgical planners whose work would bring discredit to the Church and to the one appointed to lead it, Pope Paul VI.

Therefore to effectively exonerate Paul VI, it is necessary to point out the true culprits of this plan, lest we keep barking up the wrong tree. The subversion of the Holy Roman Church was no one-man-job, but involved a swarm of periti that were brought in to shape the Council reform. But it is appropriate nonetheless to focus on the Bugnini cabal, since it was the eye of this conciliar hurricane that would later uproot the Faith and blow the Barque of Peter off its course.

The liturgical reform was initially spawned by the [3] *Preparatory Commission on the Liturgy* that was established on June 6, 1960, which was the original think-tank for the new Mass. Not everyone on the Commission was radical-left, including the President of the Commission, Cardinal Gaetano Cicognani and his successor Cardinal Larraona, who exerted strong conservative pull on the board. But the modernists unfortunately exerted greater control and were able to blueprint a new Mass, incorporating conservative ideas for cosmetic purposes only.

---

[3]   *This was originally sanctioned by John XXIII with the view that it should lead to a deeper appreciation of the old liturgy. There were no designs in his plan to make changes to the Mass, but Bugnini quickly changed this plan unbeknownst to him. Cardinal Heenan of Westminster even said in his autobiography that "Pope John did not suspect what was being planned by the liturgical experts."*

In 1960 Msgr. Bugnini was tragically placed in a position that enabled him to exert profound influence on the history of the Church when he was appointed Secretary of the Preparatory Commission. With his position and reputation as a liturgist he was then able to recruit dissident theologians to his side, whereupon they together drafted what has come to be known as the "Bugnini Schema" on the Mass.

Before the liturgical schema could be presented at the Second Vatican Council for debate, it first had to be approved and signed by Cardinal Cicognani who headed the Commission. But when it was submitted to him for approval on February 1, 1962, he immediately detected that the schema contained grave doctrinal dangers that could grow into something disastrous and was having grave misgivings about signing it. So Bugnini immediately arranged for pressure to be placed on Cicognani by having the Vatican [4]Secretary of State come to the Commission and speak to him with words of persuasion.

One can only imagine the great diabolical pressures being placed on him at that time. The entire assembly of hell must have been present exerting their fullest powers against him, since his signature would put the schema through and open the way for the destruction of the Catholic Church. With the old cardinal practically in tears he finally waved the document in the air and said out loud: "They want me to sign this but I don't know if I want to!" Then he laid the document on his desk, picked up a pen, and signed it. Four days later he died. *(The Rhine Flows into the Tiber)*

Cicognani's signature was the button that launched Bugnini's designs, without which his plans for a new Mass would have been in ruins. Consider Bugnini's own words: "If Cardinal Cicognani had not signed the Constitution, humanly speaking it would have been a disaster." (Annibale Bugnini, *La Riforma Liturgica,* 1983)

---

[4] *The Secretariat just happened to be Cicognani's blood brother, Cardinal Amleto Cicognani, who Bugnini skillfully called upon as a mediator for ending this liturgical filibuster.*

What is interesting is that Bugnini was dismissed from two important posts a short time after his schema on the Mass was approved. Through the intervention of Cardinal Larraona, the new head of the Commission, Pope John XXIII got wise to Bugnini's destructive intentions and sinister connections, and had him removed from his chair at the Lateran University where he taught liturgy and also from his secretaryship to the Liturgical Commission that was to oversee the schema during the conciliar debates. Unfortunately his schema on the Mass remained in force without being overturned. (Michael Davies, *How the Liturgy Fell Apart: The Enigma of Archbishop Bugnini*)

Now that the Bugnini Schema was saved, the next step was to present it at the Second Vatican Council for discussion that would take place on October 16, 1962. There were actually 72 prepared schemas up for discussion, all of which were orthodox and worthy of use, whereas the Bugnini Schema was the corrupt one of the set, being embedded with anti-church subtleties. Yet the Bugnini Draft was the one that received rave reviews from the Council while all the others were dumped and never considered! Archbishop Lefebvre who was on the Central Preparatory Commission for checking and overseeing all the Council documents had this to say:

"From the very first days, the Council was besieged by the progressive forces. We experienced it, felt it.... We had the impression that something abnormal was happening and this impression was rapidly confirmed; fifteen days after the opening session not one of the [5] seventy-two schemas remained. All had been sent back, rejected, thrown into the waste-paper basket....

---

[5]   *The 72 schemas were actually reduced to 20 in number, but because they were so radically altered, they no longer constituted the same documents, so that what Lefebvre said holds true: that all 72 schemas were rejected and never used. Only the Bugnini Schema survived untouched. From that point counter-schemas were drafted which grew into the 16 documents of Vatican II.*

"The immense work that had been found accomplished was scrapped and the assembly found itself empty-handed, with nothing ready." (Archbishop Lefebvre, *Open Letter to Confused Catholics,* 1986)

The 72 schemata was the original outline for Vatican II that John XXIII and his theologians had spent over two years preparing before the Council. According to Lefebvre, the 72 schemas were conservative and orthodox and should have been used, and he deplored the fact that the Council fathers rejected them after they had received the necessary one-third vote to get them approved. The Rhine fathers protested the passage of the schemata, saying, "This is inadmissible!" They abhorred the orthodoxy of the preparatory outline with its strict formulations and resented the idea of having it imposed upon them by a pope who "clung to the old absolute traditions."

Pope John, fearing a tumult, backed down and consented to let the Rhine fathers have their way against game rules. Though he had planned it differently, the fear of creating a ruckus apparently got the better of him. Hence what was being called the most meticulous and painstaking preparation ever undertaken for any council of Church history was suddenly dumped to the glee of this Council confederacy. Only the liturgical schema remained, and this in turn would be enhanced by additional counter-schemas that they would draft along the same lines.

This is why the Rhine fathers spearheaded the coup at the opening of the Council, so that they could control what was discussed and approved. With some arm twisting they were able to scrap Pope John's plan and draft up their own plan. And the rest is history. The Bugnini Schema on the Mass would now be the focus of the Council which would become the Constitution on the Sacred Liturgy, and this would set into motion a new order of change that would radically alter the course of Church history.

It was this stormy road ahead that Paul VI would bewail for the rest of his life. His retrospect on the Council is what would later compel him to confess that the smoke of satan had entered the Church.

A Second Look at the Pauline Pontificate

The reign of Paul VI was a grueling obstacle course of thorns and contradictions during which his performance as pope improved with the passing of time. It was a brutal live-and-learn experience, though his wisdom and instruction were not always reflected in his administration, thanks to the misrepresentation of his subjects. Had his cardinals been loyal to him, he conceivably could have appeared as illustrious as Pius XII and his predecessors.

However Paul VI did make some mistakes for which he had to endure heavy penance, though the intention behind these moves rendered them minor as far as moral violation is concerned. Unfortunately he had to learn the hard way that trusting the wrong people was not the right thing to do.

Perhaps the biggest mistake of his pontificate was when he reopened the [6] Vatican II Council on September 29, 1963, after it had closed down upon the death of John XXIII on June 3rd. Pope John had never intended Vatican II to go beyond December of 1962. This is one of the reasons he cried out on his deathbed to "Stop the Council!" His urgent plea was witnessed only by his closest aides who unfortunately concealed the matter very carefully, so that the majority of cardinals were not aware of it, including Cardinal Giovanni Montini who would become Pope Paul VI on June 21, 1963.

---

6   *For the record, Vatican II was not a dogmatic council which means that its documents and pronouncements were not infallible. Cardinal Ratzinger [later Benedict XVI] told the bishops of Chili in 1988: "The truth is that this particular Council defined no dogma at all...and yet many treat it as though it had made itself into a sort of super-dogma which takes away the importance of all the rest." Pope Paul VI likewise cited the non-infallible status of Vatican II when he said that the Council "avoided issuing solemn dogmatic definitions backed by the Church's infallible teaching authority." (Speaking at the general audience, December 1, 1966)*

Montini had never been in favor of having a Council to begin with, but with the help of ecumenical salesmen and conciliar sweet-talkers coupled with his own pastoral aspirations, he was convinced to reopen Vatican II that September, thinking he would be assisting a noble effort to reach the world with the message of Christ. However he would have never reopened the Council had he known of Pope John's urgent request to close it down.

Pope Paul was actually at odds with the progressive element at the Council, though his charity didn't always permit him to see this division. The pope on one hand was deeply pastoral with a passionate desire to see the whole world drawn to the bosom of the Church for its salvation. His opening speech at the second session of Vatican II addressed this very issue of the Church's pastoral mission. Accordingly, he was sincere and trusting.

Vatican II progressives on the other hand had no intention of drawing the world to the Catholic Church. They were just plain worldly in their aspirations. The idea of converting outsiders to the Catholic Church repulsed them, but they somehow had a way of making the pope think that *their* aspirations were *his* aspirations, even saying things like, "Yes, Holy Father, we want to assist your efforts to reach the world so we can all be one in Christ." But their aspiration was to join the world in its merry-making, unlike Pope Paul's which was to bring the lost sheep of this world back to the Catholic Church.

Unfortunately the pope was taken with their false proposals of peace and brotherhood where he agreed to keep the doors of the Council open to outsiders, thinking falsely that a genuine program of evangelization was underway. No doubt these proposals of peace rang in the Holy Father's ears, which only added to his misery later when it dawned on him that the Father of liars had reared its head at the Council to make war. The candy-scented smoke from his nostrils somehow had seeped through the conciliar cracks and deluded the cardinals with this new "aggiornamento."

However by the end of the third session which adjourned in November 1964, the pope had gone from being naïve and

& Fitness Trackers, Tech/electronics, fine watches, post-season team merchandise, baby gear, cause-related merchandise and other charitable items, gift cards, salon products, mEYEwear department, services, special orders (except furniture), designer handbags & shoes from select brands (such as, but not limited to, Vera Bradley, Donald Pliner, Frye; see right for full listing). **Excludes** merchandise from adidas, BLANKNYC, Breville, Brookstone, Calvin Klein Performance, Chaser, Coach accessories & footwear, Columbia, Discovery Kids, Dooney & Bourke, Dyson, FAO Schwarz, Fossil Q, Free People, Hallmark, Hart Schaffner Marx, Jordan, Juicy Couture apparel, Kate Spade, Kenneth Cole ladies', Levi's, LXR & Co, Mattel, Melissa & Doug, Michael Kors/MICHAEL Michael Kors ladies', Michael Kors men's sportswear, Moroccanoil, Movado, Mud Pie, Nike, NYDJ, PUMA, Ralph Lauren/Polo men's & kids' apparel, Ray-Ban, Sanctuary, Splendid, Swarovski, Tempur-Pedic, Tommy Bahama, Tommy Hilfiger Sport, UGG, Under Armour, Vietri, Villeroy & Boch, and Wacoal.

C00000

ONLINE PROMO CO[

While supplies last. Cannot be used on top of other coupons or "use car[
one coupon discount may be applied per item.** Coupon will not be available[
will not be honored. Valid in store or online. Cannot be applied to previous purcha[
and mattresses, Clearance Centers, Tech/electronics, kitchen electrics, personal &[

unassuming, to more enlightened and exercised in matters of spiritual warfare. His superlative speech on the devil given on November 15, 1972, was like no other given by a previous pope. His school was Vatican bureaucracy, coupled with the Divine Paraclete, Who was pointing out to him the spiritual traps that were being set by the advocates of the new church.

The document "Lumen Gentium" was an insidious work of deception which, under the pretext of presenting the Church's light to the world, was aimed at undermining the Church's hierarchical structure by redefining the priesthood as the "People of God" constituted by the "gathering of two or more in his name," which was now understood to extend into other religions beyond the limits of the institutionalized Church of Rome. And whereas the pope wouldn't quite let himself see it this way, being polite, trusting, and gracious as he was, neither did he buy its anti-clerical theme which "defied the Council."

They wanted Pope Paul to endorse this document, but before he did he issued an explanatory note to be inserted therein which confirmed the Primacy of Peter, a step which was viewed by many as meddling in the affairs of the Council. The pope said in his note: "As Supreme Pastor of the Church, the Supreme Pontiff can always exercise his power at will, as his very office demands." He said the College of Cardinals "acts as a college in the strict sense only from time to time and only with the consent of its head." For obvious reasons his statement stirred heated debate among the Council fathers.

There was also a move at the third session to contest the Virgin Mary's intercessory role and strip her of her titles, so the pope counteracted this by drafting his own statement on Mariology and included it as the last chapter of Lumen Gentium, which embarrassed many of the Council fathers. As they saw it, he was infecting their "venerable" document with his own "medieval" ideas which they argued should be treated as a separate document. But the pope's objective here was to use the document to extol the cause of the Blessed Virgin, not their cause.

It is in this last chapter of Lumen Gentium that the document lives up to its title by showing how Mary is that powerful Mediatrix of Heaven through which the light of God is shined upon the human race for its enlightenment. The Catholic Church of course is that "Lumen Gentium" through which mankind is enlightened and brought to the vision of God, but it is through Mary that this is done. It is the pure and radiant soul of Mary that reflects this heavenly light in our direction, so that the mysteries of God which otherwise would be obscure and beyond our reach are now clarified and made accessible.

What the Blessed Virgin said in Holy Scripture applies: "My soul doth magnify the Lord!" (Luke 1: 49) She is that heavenly intercessor through whom the light of God is magnified. "She is the brightness of eternal light, and the unspotted mirror of God's majesty, and the image of his goodness." (Wisdom 7: 26)

Pope Paul's objective in the document was to show that Mary is the true Lumen Gentium that God has given the world for its illumination, that She is that powerful Mediatrix from on high who alone can dispense to the world the true image and doctrine of Her Son, and without whom the world can never know the true Christ. He in fact was refuting Protestant doctrine by showing that Mary is the Mother of the Church who has been given full custody over man's salvation.

With this very point in mind, Pope Paul concluded the third session on November 21, 1964, by pronouncing Mary the *Mother of the Church.* In his closing speech to the cardinals, he said: "This year, the homage of our Council appears much more precious and significant. By the promulgation of today's constitution, which has as its crown and summit a whole chapter dedicated to Our Lady, we can rightly affirm that the present session ends as an incomparable hymn of praise in honor of Mary."

The foregoing declaration nicely reflects his penned statement on Mariology which is worth taking a look at. The following is from chapter eight of Lumen Gentium which was written solely by Pope Paul VI.

61. Predestined from eternity by that decree of divine providence which determined the incarnation of the Word to be the Mother of God, the Blessed Virgin was on this earth the Virgin Mother of the Redeemer, and above all others and in a singular way the generous associate and humble handmaid of the Lord. She conceived, brought forth and nourished Christ. She presented Him to the Father in the temple, and was united with Him by compassion as He died on the Cross. In this singular way she cooperated by her obedience, faith, hope and burning charity in the work of the Saviour in giving back supernatural life to souls. Wherefore she is our mother in the order of grace.

62. This maternity of Mary in the order of grace began with the consent which she gave in faith at the Annunciation and which she sustained without wavering beneath the cross, and lasts until the eternal fulfillment of all the elect. Taken up to heaven she did not lay aside this salvific duty, but by her constant intercession continued to bring us the gifts of eternal salvation. By her maternal charity, she cares for the

brethren of her Son, who still journey on earth surrounded by dangers and cultics, until they are led into the happiness of their true home. Therefore the Blessed Virgin is invoked by the Church under the titles of Advocate, Auxiliatrix, Adjutrix, and Mediatrix....

66. Placed by the grace of God, as God's Mother, next to her Son, and exalted above all angels and men, Mary intervened in the mysteries of Christ and is justly honored by a special cult in the Church. Clearly from earliest times the Blessed Virgin is honored under the title of Mother of God, under whose protection the faithful took refuge in all their dangers and necessities. Hence after the Synod of Ephesus the cult of the people of God toward Mary wonderfully increased in veneration and love, in invocation and imitation, according to her own prophetic words: "All generations shall call me blessed, because He that is mighty hath done great things to me". This cult, as it always existed, although it is altogether singular, differs essentially from the cult of adoration which is offered to the Incarnate Word, as well to the Father and the Holy Spirit, and it is most favorable to it. The various forms of piety toward the Mother of God, which the Church within the limits of sound and orthodox doctrine, according to the conditions of time and place, and the nature and ingenuity of the faithful has approved, bring it about that while the Mother is honored, the Son, through whom all things have their being and in whom it has pleased the Father that all fullness should dwell, is rightly known, loved and glorified and that all His commands are observed.

67. This most Holy Synod deliberately teaches this Catholic doctrine and at the same time admonishes all the sons of the Church that the cult, especially the liturgical cult, of the Blessed Virgin, be generously fostered, and the practices and exercises of piety, recommended by the Magisterium of the Church toward her in the course of centuries be made of great moment, and those decrees, which have been given in the early days regarding the cult of images of Christ, the Blessed Virgin and the saints, be religiously observed.

Given in Rome at St. Peter's on November 21, 1964.

Pope Paul's statement on Mariology was a wonderful and unexpected twist in the course of Vatican II that helped to thwart the leftist element and place things in a proper light. Unfortunately his action stoked the flames of envy that were already flaring against him. There was much murmuring among the cardinals concerning how his statements and decrees were developing independently of them, a disloyalty which was bringing undue pressure upon him.

It was these and other like battles endured for the cause that deepened Pope Paul's conviction and insight about the devil in the Church. He was battling issues on various fronts, everything from women's rights to priestly celibacy. But the major battle would center on the reform of the Liturgy, which unfortunately was already well advanced and virtually beyond his control.

The advocates of reform had much going for them at that time, since the decaying moral fabric of society was providing a good excuse to change the Catholic Church. Europe was already losing the Faith, with the age of scientific advancement waging its assault upon the human race. Everything from TV to sports, to bathing suits to cars, to movies and aspirations of wealth was captivating the hearts of men and drawing them away from the Apostolic Faith. So there was a certain need to renew the Faith by re-shining the light of Tradition over our bedimmed planet, that it might attract men of good will back to the fold. And naturally the progressives realized this; they knew they had a good *pitch* in their hands. The liturgy would be their tool.

Leftists Playing Their Advantage

Now the Freemasons and their progressivist pawns were present at Vatican II. And their objective was to build a new church of man that advocated unity and oneness with the world, not with God. But they knew that if they could do this under the guise of a renewal where "active participation" was the big issue, it would go over big at the Council, both with modernists seeking unity with the world, and with conservatives seeking renewed unity with God. For they knew that if the conciliar documents were worded ambiguously where liberal proposals were given a certain appearance of orthodoxy, even orthodox clergy would interpret them to mean that the Council was calling us to renew our allegiance to Tradition.

This might especially go over with those of strong pastoral aspiration to see society actively renewed in the propagation of the true Faith. Pope Paul initially believed that the Council would be a spur to enhance the light of holy tradition for the renewed illumination of our darkening world. This in fact would have been the case had the cardinals submitted to Pope John's plan that was initially presented to the Council. But what should have happened never happened, to the great disappointment of those pious dreamers that were waiting for it to happen.

This is what Pope Paul meant in his public confession of June 29, 1972, when he said: "We believed that after the Council would come a day of sunshine in the history of the Church. But instead there has come a day of clouds and storms, and of darkness of searching and uncertainties." The pope, speaking on behalf of other disappointed Catholics, was expressing his let-down that the reform hadn't panned out, but had only produced the fools gold of novelty and all the spiritual deficit that comes with it. It was not the wished for renewal that many a good Catholic had expected. But what did they expect?

There was no need to renew the Church in 1962. The Church's doctrine and Liturgical Constitution were in perfect shape at that time, and needed no renewing. The big temptation at Vatican II was the suggestion that the Church's liturgy somehow was inadequate and that it needed to be "updated" to meet the needs of times. The Church was doubting its own Tradition and seeking change under the guise of "restoration," as we see reflected in Sacrosanctum Concilium: "Holy Mother Church desires to undertake with great care a general restoration of the liturgy itself." (21) Pius XII prophesied this infidelity while still a cardinal:

"The day will come when the civilized world will deny its God, when the Church will doubt as Peter doubted." (Cardinal Pacelli speaking in response to the Third Secret, 1931)

Doubting Tradition was not the answer to reviving the Faith, but trusting it was. "Prove all things; hold fast that which is good." (1 Thessalonians 5:21) What needed renewing at Vatican II was the resolution of the clergy to adhere more strictly to the old Constitution and teachings, and unfortunately some believed that the conciliar reform would lead them to that. Even Pope Paul had reposed such hopes initially, which was a slight mistake on his part.

The major [7]mistake he made, aside from reopening Vatican II, was when he appointed Annibale Bugnini to head the new Consilium on the Liturgy in February of 1964, since the plan of Bugnini and his cohorts was to use the liturgy as their tool to destroy the Catholic Church. Pope Paul would have never appointed Bugnini had he known what he was to learn of him later (see chapter 7). Obviously he didn't know the true reason for his dismissal in 1962, if in fact he knew anything of it at all. The reason for his dismissal was that he was a "progressivist" and an "iconoclast," which were the accusations then being echoed by the Congregation of Rites and the Holy Office, with "innuendos whispered half-aloud." (Michael Davies, *Liturgical Time Bombs in Vatican II*)

But Bugnini's exile was basically kept at a hush with the help of his comrades on the Commission who were able to keep the work going in his absence. With their sphere of influence they managed to keep the matter of Bugnini's discharge at a low-key so that when the matter of his new appointment was later proposed to Pope Paul, he naively complied with their plan, trusting that Bugnini would carry out his commission in good faith. Unfortunately Bugnini was a deceiver, and the docile pope fell prey to his wile by consenting to the appointment.

---

7   *Not in the moral sense, but in the sense of proper judgment. However, the pope later judged correctly that Bugnini was conspiratorial so that he had him removed from the Congregation of Divine Worship.*

Perfidious Murmurings

But during the course of the Council, Pope Paul grew increasingly disturbed at discussions circulating about new formulas for the Mass which were surfacing more and more with the implementative process underway. Though he initially had reposed hope in the reform, even contributing somewhat, he was never attempting to breach Tradition or invent a New Mass, and did not agree with these new formulas being proposed.

Toward the end of Vatican II he said: "There are some who with reference either to Masses which are celebrated in private, or to the Dogma of Transubstantiation, or to devotion to the Eucharist, spread abroad opinions which disturb the faithful and fill their minds with no little confusion about matters of faith. It is as if everyone were permitted to consign to oblivion doctrine already defined by the Church." (September 3, 1965)

Pope Paul here was refuting Vatican infidels who mocked the Mystery of Faith as superstition and who were opposed to the idea of private Masses on the grounds that they undermined the new conciliar priority of communal activity, a trend that was taking precedence over everything else. According to these secular humanists, Mass was not Mass unless it was an occasion of festive human encounter, to which Pope Paul sharply disagreed, saying, "It is not allowable to emphasize what is called the 'communal' Mass to the disparagement of Masses celebrated in private…. Nor is it allowable to discuss the mystery of Transubstantiation without mentioning what the Council of Trent stated about the marvelous conversion of the whole substance of the bread into the Body and of the whole substance of the wine into the Blood of Christ."

The pope also refuted those who spoke of "transignification" and "transfinalization," and who proposed "the opinion according to which, in the Consecrated Hosts which remain after the celebration of the Sacrifice of the Mass, Christ Our Lord is no longer present." He warned that "the spread of these and similar

The Traditional Latin Mass with the priest facing the altar is the liturgical formula that was restated by the Council of Trent and finalized by Pius V along with a papal mandate that any attempts to modify this formula would "incur the wrath of Almighty God and of the blessed Apostles Peter and Paul." (Quo Primum, July 14, 1570) Aside from the addition of new feast days, the Rite of the Mass itself had not changed in nearly fourteen centuries. Moreover, Paul VI never abrogated the old Mass and he even stated before the end of Vatican II that the formula used by the Council of Trent "must be religiously preserved."

opinions does great harm to the faith and devotion to the Divine Eucharist," stating that "we cannot approve the opinions which they express, and we have the duty to warn you about the grave danger which these opinions involve for correct faith."

It was in his encyclical "Mysterium Fidei" that these culminating concerns were addressed for the purpose of warding off these ideas that were threatening the Faith. Therein he opposed the liturgical reform as it was being proposed, and upheld the Mass of the Council of Trent on the grounds that it alone is the formula to be used in the Roman Rite for proposing the Mystery of Faith.

The point of the encyclical was to bring into focus the sublime mystery of the Holy Eucharist as the center-piece of our Faith and how the Church may never resort to flippant or careless wording in proposing such mysteries, lest we give rise to irreverent and scandalous notions concerning the Holy Sacrifice *(e.g. the Eucharist is holy bread, the Mass is a meal, the Mass is a community gathering, the Mass is a celebration, etc).* With this premise being established, he goes on to say:

"The Church, therefore, with the long labor of centuries and the help from the Holy Ghost has established a rule of language [Tridentine Liturgy], confirming it with the authority of the Councils. This rule which has often been the watchword and banner of orthodox Faith must be religiously preserved.... Let no one presume to change it at his own pleasure or under the pretext of new knowledge. Who would ever tolerate that the dogmatic formulas used by the ecumenical councils for the mysteries of the Holy Trinity and the Incarnation be judged as no longer appropriate for men of our times and therefore that other formulas be rashly substituted for them? In the same way, it cannot be tolerated that any individual should on his own authority modify the formulas used by the Council of Trent to propose the Eucharistic Mystery for our belief.... These formulas are adapted to all men of all times and all places." *(Pope Paul VI, September 3, 1965)*

Though it is not common knowledge, it was determined in 1986 by a panel of nine cardinals from the Curia that Pope Paul VI never abrogated the Mass of Pius V, nor did he mandate the New Mass, nor did he ever grant bishops the right to forbid or restrict priests from saying the Tridentine Latin Mass. The Mass of Pius V remains in force to this day according to their finding. Pope John Paul II had commissioned the cardinals to look into the legal status of the Old Mass, as it was his intention to bring its legality to light.

This in turn laid the groundwork for Benedict XVI to continue the process of liberating the old rite when he issued his Moto Proprio on the Latin Mass on July 7, 2007, reaffirming the legality of the pre-conciliar Latin Mass. The Moto Proprio didn't actually make the Old Mass legal but made official what already was the case, thereby declaring that it always was the right of priests to say the Old Mass without permission from their bishops. After all, if priests today do not need permission to say a Mass that was never mandated, then they certainly don't need permission to say the Mass that was.

If Pope Paul VI had truly mandated the New Mass he would have specified this, but this was never done. Pius V, on the contrary, laid down the law with his subjects in his July, 1570, Constitution on the Mass, saying, "We order them in virtue of holy obedience to chant or to read the Mass according to the rite and manner and norm herewith laid down by Us." He said: "Let Masses not be sung or read according to any other formula than that of this Missal published by Us" mandating that "This new rite alone is to be used."

In the April 1969 *Missale Romanum,* which is the Apostolic Constitution for the promulgation of the Novus Ordo, there is no such mandate for the New Mass or that it should even be used. The document merely mandates the publication of the new missal with its revised text, ordering that "the prescriptions of this Constitution go into effect November 30th of this year" and that it "be firm and effective now and in the future." But there is no mention of its use.

The decree then validates and makes available the new missal for those who want it. A Traditionalist priest of the Society of St. Pius X, Father Francois Laisney, points out that "Pope Paul VI did not oblige the use of his [new] Mass, but only permitted it.... There is no clear order, command, or precept imposing it on any priest!" According to Fr. Laisney, the same applies to subsequent decrees on the New Mass, including the 1971 Notification from the Congregation of Divine Worship, of which he says: "One cannot find in this text any clear prohibition for any priest to use the traditional Mass nor an obligation to celebrate only the New Mass."

Father Laisney speaks a pure sentence here. In order for a mandate to exist it must be stated what the mandate is. If a centuries old practice is going to be changed and imposed upon the Universal Church that will radically alter the worship of millions, then this needs to be spelled out in clear, juridical terms. Without this done there is no mandate.

The fact that a practice is universally adopted by all the Catholic bishops does not make it a mandate, nor does it necessarily constitute the ordinary practice or teaching of the Church. The Arian Heresy of the fourth century also had the unanimous backing of the Catholic bishops, and it in fact was mandated upon the people, but there was nothing ordinary about it. "Wrong is wrong even if everyone is doing it," says St. Augustine. The Church's ordinary precepts, as with dogma, are something that God Himself has to bless and guide through His Vicar on earth. This blessing was never given for the New Mass. The blessing was merely permissive in allowing the true blessing of the Latin Mass to be put aside momentarily.

The fact is that Paul VI was against the radical changes in the Mass, but there was little he could do about it since the plan to change the Mass was already in full swing, and proposals to the contrary were seen as an infringement at this point. By 1967 there were even plans in the works to strip the canon of the Mass to the point of rendering it a mere communion service, and they were hoping to use Pope Paul's signature to get it promulgated. And whereas the pope did sign for the [8]New Mass in April 1969, he wasn't going to do it until it was first brought up to code with the insertion of some counter-reforms including his own Eucharistic prayer no. 1, so that the faithful could at least have a valid Mass to attend.

The pope's performance during this time was not perfect, granted, but by constantly being pressured by innovators who were trying to exact reforms and signatures out of him, he

---

[8]   *Though defective in its formulas, the Mass in the new rite remains valid in that the Sacrifice of Calvary thereby is reenacted, as in the Tridentine Rite. The holiness or disposition of the priest has nothing to do with the validity of the Mass, provided the priest is legally ordained and that the essentials of Consecration (This is My Body - This is My Blood) remain intact, which they are today. The problem with the New Mass is not its validity, but its scandalous nature in the way it causes people to think more of man than of God. Those attending the Novus Ordo should use the old Missal and remain kneeling throughout the Mass, especially from the Sanctus to the final blessing.*

eventually started to weaken where he would even force himself to adopt their arguments of reform in order to console himself, seeing that the coming change was inevitable. And too, he was holding on to his dream that the reform was going to renew the ancient fervor of the Church.

But in his heart he knew the changes were immoral and that they would rob the Church of this very participation in the Mystery of God which it had enjoyed through the ages. Consider his lamentation over the coming promulgation of the New Mass which he delivered at the General Audience of November 26, 1969:

"Newness is going to be noticed, the newness of language. No longer Latin, but the spoken language will be the principal language of the Mass. The introduction of the vernacular will certainly be a *great sacrifice* for those who know the beauty, the power, and the expressive sacrality of Latin. We are parting with the speech of the Christian centuries; we are becoming like profane intruders in the literary preserve of sacred utterance. We will lose a great part of that stupendous and incomparable artistic and spiritual thing, the Gregorian chant. We have reason for regret, reason almost for bewilderment. What can we put in the place of that language of the Angels? We are giving up something of priceless worth. But why? What is more precious than these loftiest of our Church's values?"

Clearly the pope did not like the switch to vernacular. Later in his talk he went on to acknowledge that, yes, we cannot effectively reach people with the Gospel if we start speaking to them in a strange tongue (Latin), and he asserts that we must speak to people in their own language if we want to communicate to them. But his point was that when we speak to Almighty God in the Sacrifice of the Mass, we must speak His language. For in the Mass we speak to God, not to one another.

The use of Latin is an essential part of the eternal plan to maintain ecclesiastical unity and strength, since the Church is of one universal faith, doctrine, and language. Therefore the switch to vernacular after the Council was a major contributing factor to the present day disunity in the Church, because with the Mass said today in the language of each country, this has fostered the idea that the Church is something that is secular and divided, as opposed to holy and universal. So a return to the old Latin Rite is needed to restore unity to the Church as it existed before Vatican II.

And not just the Latin, but the whole package. The Masonic plan against the Church was to strip it of its beauty and majesty so that it would no longer be that effective instrument to inspire and attract mankind to the heart of God. This is why the conversions from Judaism and Islam have drastically dropped since Vatican II, because reform made the Church ugly.

Christ gave us His Church that it might be a light to the nations signified by that Latin word, *Lumen Gentium*. The light of Tradition emanating from the Old Rite is that *Lumen Gentium* wherewith to attract the world to Christ, but by withholding this light from the world the Church in our time is hindering the plan for man's salvation. This is why Pope Paul said "we have reason for regret, reason almost for bewilderment." What Our Lady prophesied at La Salette has truly come to pass: "The Church will be in eclipse, the world will be in dismay." (1846)

Early Roots of Reform

If there is any one thing that we can pinpoint as the cause of the liturgical revolution, it is the convocation of the Second Vatican Council in 1962, something that Cardinal Montini was not in favor of. In fact, when he heard in January 1959 that Pope John XXIII had announced his convocation of the Council, he actually expressed his alarm over this and said: "This old boy does not know what a hornet's nest he is stirring up!" (CBC News) The hornets of reform saw Vatican II as their opening to come in and create a buzz in the Holy City. This was the "fissure" through which the progressivist alliance would break through with their reform of the Mass.

However the plan to destroy the Mass goes back many centuries and didn't just happen overnight. Luther, who founded the reformist movement, understood keenly that the way to destroy the Church is by destroying the Mass upon which the entire Church is built. "It is indeed upon the Mass as on a rock that the whole papal system is built, with its monasteries, its bishoprics, its collegiate churches, its altars, its ministries, its doctrine, i.e., with all its guts. All these cannot fail to crumble once their sacrilegious and abominable Mass falls." (Martin Luther, *Against Henry, King of England*, 1522, Werke, Vol. X, p. 220.)

Martin Luther

The Council of Trent convened from 1545-1563 to condemn Luther and the Reformation and to mandate once and forever the formula for the Mass. The Council put the dog out as it were, so that reformers from that point were forced to operate outside the Church, barking at a distance, while the Church enjoyed that safeguard and liberty that came through the old liturgical formula.

But when they convened the Second Vatican Council the dog came back in, something that Montini suspected would happen from the onset. It was for reason that Popes Pius X, XI, and XII had all refrained from calling an ecumenical council, because they knew it would provide an opening for the progressivist Rhine coalition that had been building its forces against the Church.

The major thrust of the Alliance was to revive the cause of Martin Luther who denied the supernatural presence of Christ in the Eucharist and who insisted that Christians are unconditionally saved regardless of their sins. His war against the Catholic priesthood would now be assisted by Vatican II. The 1980 Joint Catholic-Lutheran Commission which grew out of Vatican II even states: "Among the ideas of the Second Vatican Council, we can see gathered together much of what Luther asked for, such as the following: description of the Church as 'The People of God'; accent on the priesthood of all baptized; the right of the individual to freedom of religion."

This Reformationalist plan to strip the old Mass and revive Luther's lay empowerment concept is seen in article 50 of *Sacrosanctum Concilium* which is the finalized version of the Constitution on the Sacred Liturgy, issued on December 4, 1963. Therein it states that archaic "elements" accumulated through time "are now to be discarded" and "the rites are to be simplified" so that "active participation by the faithful may be more easily achieved."

These are among the very ideas that Pope Paul did not agree with. He maintained that sacred "elements" accumulated through time "must be religiously preserved," not "discarded," and insisted that the rites not be simplified or changed "under the pretext of new knowledge." Pope Paul was a pure Roman, and was not of the heretical Rhine school that was attempting to bring back Martin Luther. As he told the French Philosopher, Jean Guitton:

"What strikes me when I think of the Catholic world is that within Catholicism there seems sometimes to predominate a non-Catholic way of thinking, and it can happen that this non-Catholic thought within Catholicism will tomorrow become the stronger. But it will never represent the thought of the Church. It is necessary that a small flock subsist, no matter how small it might be." (Jean Guitton, *Paul VI Secret,* 1979)

It was the reformers of deceit, and not Pope Paul, that penned the Concilium which states that "elements which have suffered injury through accidents of history are now to be restored." (50) By this the modernists were venting their complaint about the injury suffered by Luther and the Reformation through their expulsion by the Council of Trent, which the conciliar elite lamented as an unfortunate "accident of history."

Cardinal Adrianus Simonis, the former Primate of the Netherlands, spoke of a *Second Reformation* underway in the Church that is on par with the 16th century movement that lacerated Christianity, saying that, "it is even more dangerous today." He says it is a crisis "which has penetrated deep in the Church," a danger "we must fight with our eyes wide open" because "the very foundations of the Faith are being questioned." He also said:

"Paul VI was right when he said that there was a risk that non-Catholic thinking was prevailing in the Catholic Church. I found it remarkable that he had been aware of this danger all those years ago when so few recognize it today." (EWTN 1996)

That Vatican II was instrumental in renewing the principles of the Protestant Reformation in the Catholic Church is evidenced by the words of Fr. Edward Schillebeeckx, a noted Belgian theologian and prominent figure of the Council, when he remarked: "One is astonished to find oneself more in sympathy with the thinking of Christian, non-Catholic 'observers' than with the views of one's own brethren on the other side of the dividing line. The accusation of connivance with the Reformation is therefore not without foundation." The accusation indeed is justified. Fr. Schillebeeckx was of that infamous Rhine group that overtook Vatican II, and the reform they advocated was in fact rooted in Luther's Reformation.

One of their key objectives was to redefine the priesthood as *The People of God.* Their philosophy was that the Church is one hierarchy or priesthood but in different ranks, with the ordained priesthood being only one rank of this priesthood. "The People of God is not only an assembly of various peoples, but in itself is made up of different ranks." (Lumen Gentium, 13) What is promoted here is the fallacy that we are all priests of one hierarchy.

"The [9] common priesthood of the faithful and the ordained priesthood are nonetheless ordered one to another; each in its own proper way shares in the one priesthood of Christ." (Lumen Gentium, 10)

For the record, there is no such thing as a "common priesthood of the faithful." This was Luther's idea. This terminology was used to justify their plan to have lay people perform liturgical functions as in the priesthood (e.g. Eucharistic Ministers, women lectors) to teach that the presence of Christ at Mass is brought about, not by the priest, but by the assembly of people numbering two or more, as if they collectively were the priest. This coincides with article 7 of the Vatican II Concilium: "In the liturgy the whole public worship is performed by the Mystical Body of Jesus Christ, that is, by the Head and His members."

---

[9]   *This terminology is falsely attributed to 1 Peter 2:9 which refers to the Church as "a chosen race, a royal priesthood, a holy nation." The verse about a "royal priesthood" is merely figurative to indicate the sacrificial nature of the Church, since the principal function of a priest is to offer sacrifice, so in that sense we are a sacrificial or priestly people. We are called to atone and to follow the sacrificial Lamb in His sacrificial sufferings that we might reign with Christ as "a royal priesthood, a holy nation." This verse of scripture references our call to atonement, and has nothing to do with the priestly office and its functions as the Vatican II documents deceptively imply.*

Naturally the entire Church is called to adore God with one mind, but this is not what modernist innovators meant. What they were saying is that lay people should perform the liturgy, not just the priest.

Hence it was the liturgy that modernists had been eye-balling long before the Council, since it would be the primary vessel used to advance a new church. Vatican II was their opening to slip into the Church and start making changes. The adversary knew that if he could get his foot in the door he could use the Church's liturgical apparatus as a lever to steer the Holy Barque onto a new course if the liturgy were simply altered.

This is what happened at the Council. The 1964 conciliar instruction, Inter Oecumenici, article 91, called for [10] "celebration facing the people" which diverted the Church from its path. The focus of the Council was now for "active participation by the faithful" around which everything was to revolve, as expressed in section 14 of the Concilium on the liturgy: "The full and active participation by all the people is the aim to be considered before all else." This new socialist ideal was most effectively spearheaded by the new liturgical celebration, which set the stage for the new church of man.

But again, Paul VI wasn't even pope when the Constitution on the Sacred Liturgy was drafted, nor did he appoint the engineers of reform to chair the drafting commissions. He basically inherited a whirlwind when he was elected, which unfortunately he wasn't always able to stand up against. His stalks bent in the wind somewhat, granted, and he did make some mistakes, being a bit lenient with the insubordinate ones.

---

10   *According to acclaimed liturgist, Monsignor Klaus Gamber, this was the most destructive of all the post-conciliar reforms, citing that "neither in the Eastern nor the Western Church was there ever a celebration facing the people" which he calls "a turning towards man, and away from God." (The Reform of the Roman Liturgy, 1993) Cardinal Ratzinger [later Benedict XVI] publicly praised Msgr. Gamber as a "prophet for our time" who he called "the one scholar who, among the army of pseudo liturgists, truly represents the liturgical thinking of the centre of the Church."*

But at the same time he made some heroic moves to defend the culture of life, to defend Mary the Mother of the Church, to denounce feminism and contraception, and yes, to denounce the attempts to alter the Tridentine formula for saying the Mass. The pope made this clear in his September 3, 1965, statement on the Mass: "It cannot be tolerated that any individual should on his own authority modify the formulas used by the Council of Trent to propose the Eucharistic Mystery for our belief."

By this statement the pope was not implying that the work of changing the Mass should be left up to him alone, since the very point of his encyclical was to say that the Church through the centuries "has established a rule of language" which "must be religiously preserved." Meaning, by all. He said, "Let no one presume to change it at his own pleasure or under the pretext of new knowledge." But nobody listened, consequently change ensued.

Revelations

The greatest of the approved Marian apparitions of the 20th century are those of the Virgin Mary to three shepherd children at Fatima, Portugal, which occurred on the 13th of six consecutive months beginning on May 13, 1917. On July 13 of that year the Blessed Virgin delivered to the children a great Secret, which is comprised of three distinct parts, the first two of which were released by the Church in October of 1930.

However, the third part commonly known as "The Third Secret" remains a secret, and still awaits release. But from the words of Jacinta, the youngest of the Fatima seers, we know that part of the Secret pertained to the vicious attacks on the papacy that would culminate in the year 1972, at which time the Holy Father would have much to suffer. This would mark the beginning of an extended period of persecution for the Church through which the papacy would be subdued and put in chains by dissident clergy, whereby the hierarchy would then become an instrument to mislead the Catholic faithful throughout the world.

It was this very situation that prompted Pope Paul VI to cry out in **June of 1972** that the smoke of Satan had entered the Church. What had begun ten years earlier with the subversion of Vatican II finally culminated in 1972 with this takeover of the Roman Curia, at which time the power of the papacy fell into the hands of the Secretariat of State. The same continues to control the Vatican today.

Little Jacinta told the nun caring for her on her deathbed that they **"would keep united to the Vatican to prepare for the year 1972,** because the sins of impurity, vanity, and excessive luxury would bring great chastisements to the world, which would cause great suffering to the Holy Father." Jacinta repeatedly referred to this victim pope in her visions as the **"Poor Holy Father!"**

Jacinta's revelation is documented in a letter sent to Pope Pius XII on April 25, 1954 by Mother Maria of the Purification Godinho, the nun caring for Jacinta. Jacinta died in February 1920 at the age of ten.

Jacinta also relayed one of her visions of the "Poor Holy Father" to Sister Lucy, the eldest of the Fatima seers. According to Lucy, the pope in Jacinta's vision is mentioned in the [11] Third Secret of Fatima, the same who would suffer greatly from 1972 on. The following is related by Fatima expert, Frere Michel de la Sainte Trinite, and is taken from his book, *The Third Secret of Fatima.*

---

[11] *The Third Secret was supposed to be released by 1960, but was kept hidden because of the drastic nature of the message. Among those who have read and commented on the Secret, we find a common thread in that it concerned the great apostasy of the last times and how the infiltration of heresy would begin at the top and filter down to the man in the pew. Pope John Paul II had initiated a move to release the Third Secret in June 2000, but Cardinal Sodano and the Vatican bureaucracy overtook the project so that the Secret was buried and swapped with a lengthy statement aimed at whitewashing and discrediting the Secret.*

"One day", Lucy says, "we spent our siesta down by my parents' well. Jacinta sat on the stone slabs on top of the well. Francisco and I climbed up a steep bank in search of wild honey among the brambles in a nearby thicket. After a little while, Jacinta called out to me: **"Didn't you see the Holy Father?"**

"No", Lucy answered.

"I don't know how it happened, but I saw the Holy Father in a very big house, kneeling by a table, with his head buried in his hands, and he was weeping. Outside the house, there were many people. Some of them were [12] throwing stones, others were cursing him and using bad language. Poor Holy Father, we must pray very much for him."

"One day", Lucy continues, "two priests recommended us to pray for the Holy Father, and explained to us who the Pope was. Afterwards, Jacinta asked me: **"Is he the one I saw weeping, the one Our Lady told us about in the <u>Secret</u>?"**

"Yes, he is", answered Lucy.

"The Lady must surely have shown him also to those priests."

Obviously these priests were inspired by God to know the pope's identity, and were on a mission to solicit prayers for this "Poor Holy Father" of the future. Prayers of course can be held in abeyance and used later for one's benefit, as with money or any tokens of good will. The prayers were being gathered to strengthen the Holy Father during his anguish and duress that would reach paralyzing heights in the year 1972.

---

[12] *It sometimes happens that supernatural visions are given symbolically to emphasize the point being made. This part of the vision apparently was intended to emphasize the anger and hatred that these men had for the pope.*

The Vatican Pavilion in Flushing Meadows Park, New York, was blessed by Pope Paul VI during his historic visit to America. Pilgrims gather throughout the year in witness of the Marian apparitions that occurred there during the years 1970-1995. The prayer vigils at the vigil site are conducted by SMWA under the direction of Michael Mangan (see www.smwa.org for more information).

The revelations of [13] Our Lady of the Roses to Veronica of the Cross (1970-1995) also speak of this pivotal year of 1972. According to the revelations, Pope Paul VI was the "Poor Holy Father" in Jacinta's vision. On June 8, 1978, the Blessed Virgin said: "I ask you again to pray for your Holy Father [Pope Paul VI] in Rome. He is very ill. He needs many prayers, for he is being crucified by his own. **He is truly the little one in the message of Jacinta.**"

---

[13] *These revelations were given during apparitions of the Virgin Mary that occurred from 1970-1995 at the Vatican Pavilion Site in Flushing Meadow Park, New York. While the matter still awaits ecclesiastical investigation, pilgrims gather throughout the year at the site in witness of the apparition that continues to make its impact upon the international faith community. The Vatican Pavilion is the site of the 1964-1965 New York World's Fair where Pope Paul VI gave his Apostolic blessing during his historic visit to America. Thereby the hand of providence bestowed its blessing in the anticipation of the apparitions that would follow shortly thereupon.*

Jacinta also appeared with the Virgin on that same day and told Veronica: "Yes, I tried to warn everyone of what was going to happen to the world of the future. Our Lady said that the little Father in Rome would suffer great persecution, but much of this persecution would come from his very own, those that he trusted." (Jacinta of Fatima, June 8, 1974)

On September 14, 1971, this miraculous photograph was taken of Our Lady's statue at St. Robert Bellarmine Church, the original site of the Bayside apparitions. As the photo developed, Jacinta, the child seer of Fatima, miraculously wrote from Heaven: **"Jacinta 1972."** Therein lies the heart of the famous Third Secret and the date of the coming Chastisement to man. We are instructed to examine the photo for lines, figures, and numbers.

When you exclude the letter "J," the letters remaining in Jacinta can be read: "a-c" "i-n-t-o." Turn the picture counter-clockwise and a mitre (a bishop's headpiece) is formed by the tails of the "o" and the "2" (see illustration above). Jacinta is showing us the Third Secret of Fatima: that satan, the antichrist (a-c) would enter into (i -n -t -o) many bishops and cardinals (mitres) at the highest levels of the Vatican and that 1972 would be the year that these evil forces would take over the reign of Paul VI. This good pope affirmed this on June 29, 1972: "From some fissure the smoke of satan entered into the temple of God." The Blessed Virgin herself affirmed this on September 7, 1978:

"In the city of Rome there will be great confusion and trial. Satan, Lucifer in human form, entered into Rome in the year 1972. He cut off the [14]rule, the role of the Holy Father, Pope Paul VI. Lucifer has controlled Rome and continues this control now. And I tell you, My children, unless you pray and make My counsel known to all of the ruling fathers of the Eternal City of Rome, My Son's Church, His House, would be forced into the catacombs. A great struggle lies ahead for mankind. The eventual outcome is for good of all, for this trial in My Son's Church will be a true proving ground for all the faithful. Many latter-day saints shall rise out of the tribulation."

Jacinta also appeared on February 1, 1973, and said: "All has come true as I gave to you from Our Lady, but Our Father still plans to bring you back. Everyone has so much in many things upon your earth, but yet they all look so unhappy. They are rich, and yet they are so poor. **I have come to tell you of the poor Holy Father. I cried much for him. We love him. But man will destroy him now."**

The following poem, "Exhortation," was dictated to Veronica during the vigil message of May 29, 1976, and concerns Pope Paul VI.

> *Dear Holy Father, worried and wan*
> *Will struggle with Jesus to gather the sheep.*
> *The pastures are rich, but the sheep grow thin,*
> *For the souls have succumbed to the sickness of sin.*
> *You'll need more reinforcements from Heavenly shores,*
> *So deep is the darkness of earth's shallow mores.*
> *All hearts must ascend in true supplication*
> *To avoid the sad fate of divine devastation.*
> *Dear Holy Mother, your Mother of love,*
> *Does beg you to heed these dire words from above:*
> *His heart is torn by careless surrender*
> *Of too many souls who don't try to remember.*

---

14   *That is, the power of the papacy fell into the hands of the Secretariat of State so that the Secretariat was now virtual pope of the Vatican. This lawless power would assume drastic proportions within a couple years with the emergence of a counterfeit pope in the Vatican (see chapter 9).*

The Father, the Son, the Spirit of life--
Smite in the heart by the human knife
Of hate, greed, avarice, vanity:
All indications that sin is insanity.
What more must you do now but place the full load
Of saving all souls on the few who are bold,
Who stand up and fight for all Heaven's glory
And meet with Pope Paul at the end of life's story.

Consider now the revelations allegedly given by Christ to a Mexican nun known as the little "Portavoz" messenger. The revelations were the backbone for a religious order in Mexico known as the *Franciscan Minum Nuns of the Perpetual Help of Mary* that was founded in Zamora Michoacan, Mexico, on June 24, 1942, by Mother Maria Concepcion Zuniga Lopez, with the approbation of Bishop Figicheri y Pietassanta. The Religious House is presently located at the Vergel Garden of the Immaculate Virgin of Guadalupe just outside Mexico City. The revelations were given the stamp of Imprimi Potest by Sac. Fr. J. Gaudze, m.f., Superior, on June 27, 1979. The excerpts that follow concern Pope Paul VI, and have been edited slightly to keep it concise.

March 24, 1969:

"Return to the primitive fountains of the Church. Restore the Christian and religious customs among seculars and religious, and repent, all of you who belong to the Hierarchy of My Church! All of you who have apostasized and have become traitors, repent and retrace your steps to the right way! And, of course, this must be done immediately!

"To come to Me is to confess humbly that My doctrine is holy and that it does not need reforms, that My Church is divine, and that all must come to her bosom if they wish to be saved eternally. It means to confess her royal dignity which shines through Me, from Peter to My present Vicar, My much loved Paul VI. They must obey him! Let them not pressure him, nor exact from him reforms for My Church.

"My Church is holy and I remain permanently in her, even though there should remain in her one single man who knows how to observe My doctrine purely and completely. My Church has rules of life to which all of you must subject yourselves in humble submission.

"Demagoguery, guile, error and falsehood are the tools of all those so-called sociological techniques proposed by innovators who are fighting to supplant My doctrine and My Church. All of these are brimming over with satanic evil, the evil which the spirit of Satan has infiltrated into them."

January 21, 1970

"The definitions which have been decreed from other centuries and which have been approved must not be abrogated nor changed. Let Paul VI speak the truth to the face of the world and let him confess that they have pressured him and obligated him into many present-day definitions which he in his heart has not accepted....

"Paul VI suffers! Do not leave him alone in his prison. Go in search of him! Take him out of there to a safe place where he may be able to speak freely, according to the motion and light of My Spirit. Then you shall see that he is loyal to My doctrine and that his soul overflows with charity emanating from My heart."

April 23, 1969

"My very beloved son [Pope Paul], I warn you that I am going to grant you the palm of martyrdom; but first, you will battle a great deal with the enemies of My Church and there you will begin your martyrdom. But, I advise you to free yourself from those astute men who approach you to propose aggressive movements."

One of the greatest mystics of all time is Blessed Ann Catherine Emmerich (1774-1824), an Augustinian nun who was given many visions and insights concerning the papacy in the last times before Christ's Second Coming. Consider this vision from July of 1820:

"I saw the Holy Father surrounded by traitors and in great distress about the Church. He had visions and apparitions in his hour of greatest need. I saw many good, pious Bishops; but they were weak and wavering, their cowardice often got the upper hand. I saw the Black Fellow plotting again, the destroyers attacking the Church of Peter, Mary standing with her mantle over it, and the enemies of God put to flight....Then I saw darkness spreading around and people no longer seeking the true Church. They went to one another saying: *'All is more beautiful, more natural here, better regulated':* but as yet I have seen no ecclesiastic among them."

Sister Emmerich is describing the counterfeit church of the future, so often described in her visions, that would seek to cast off Tradition and merge with other religions in a false new-world utopia of ecumenical unity. This coincides with one of the messages of Our Lady of the Roses: "You must recognize what is happening now in My Son's House. There is being rebuilt before your very eyes another religion, another church of man. No angels are helping in this building." (9-7-78) Sr. Emmerich also related the following vision:

"They built a large, singular, extravagant church which was to embrace all creeds with equal rights: Evangelicals, Catholics, and all denominations, a true communion of the unholy with one shepherd and one flock."

Sr. Emmerich speaks not of Christ, the Good Shepherd, who would eventually gather his own into one fold again, but of a wicked anti-pope of the future that would deceive the Church into merging with other religions under the guise of "peace and reconciliation." This plan to depart the True Mass and merge with world unity has been coming in steps since the Council, but the true Faith will never actually be destroyed in keeping with Christ's promise that the gates of hell will never prevail fully against his Church. (Mt. 16:18)

The infernal plan to change the Mass was prophesied over a hundred years ago by Marie Julie Jahenny, an approved mystic of the Catholic Church. Her bishop, Monsignor Fourier of Nantes, not only sanctioned but promoted her revelations, seeing that they had great spiritual value for the Church. Her message is along the same lines as the message of La Salette concerning the great apostasy and profanation of the last times, which according to the seer would bring a great and horrific punishment upon humanity.

On November 27, 1902, Our Lord announced the conspiracy to invent a "New Mass."

"I give you a warning. The disciples who are not of My Gospel are now working hard to remake according to their ideas and under the influence of the enemy of souls, a Mass that contains words that are odious in My sight! When the fatal hour arrives when the faith of my priests is put to the test, it will be these texts [new missal] that will be celebrated in this second period. The first period is the one of my priesthood which exists since Me. The second is the one of the persecution when the enemies of the Faith and of Holy Religion will impose their formulas in the book of the second celebration. Many of My holy priests will refuse this book, sealed with the words of the abyss. Unfortunately, amongst them are those who will accept it. These infamous spirits are those who crucified me and are awaiting the kingdom of the new messiah."

GIVEN THE FOREGOING REVELATIONS, Paul VI was certainly not among "these infamous spirits" that were crucifying Christ and pressing toward "the kingdom of the new messiah." The "second celebration" was not his doing, but was generated by infiltrated Freemasons working through fallen members of the hierarchy. They in turn were the ones who implemented the changes in the late sixties. The plan was to heap all the blame on the pope in order to discredit the papacy and drive the good Catholics from the Church so that these Masonic forces could get on with their *Mass destruction* without further censure. It was carefully calculated in their plan to make us think that Paul VI was the modernist culprit who masterminded the New Mass and that the Holy Sacrifice was no longer valid so that loyal Catholics would no longer feel a reason to remain in their parish churches and fight for God's glory.

Those of the Sedevacantist sect who boast of their work to expose Freemasonry fail to realize that they unknowingly are doing the work of the Freemasons to bring discredit to the papacy. Though they often mean well, they are misled in their thinking because of their deficit of grace resulting from their having separated from the main body of the Church. Christ today is being profaned by many of his own priests, therefore we do Him no favor by running off and leaving Him hanging before his enemies. St. John and the Blessed Virgin remained at the foot of the Cross despite the sacrilege and ridicule, so their example sets the stage for all the true apostles of the last days who are pressing for the restoration of the Holy Roman Catholic Church to its former glory.

The moral of the story is that if we want to win the battle, we have to remain in the arena and "let our light shine before men." Fleeing the cross and detracting the innocent is not the answer, and is certainly not in line with those champions of Tradition who defended the Faith under siege.

"From Some Fissure"

If there is one thing that describes the Catholic Church in our time, it is its sense of amnesia about the past where it discounts its own teachings about itself. Because of the influence of modernism, the Church today seems to have forgotten the basic truth of old that when a pope speaks, it is God speaking through him for our instruction. This would especially apply in the case of weighty statements of historic import that are given with a sense of urgency.

Paul VI made one such statement when he declared to the world that "from some fissure the smoke of satan entered into the temple of God." (June 29, 1972) The pope was referring to the infiltration of satanic influence whereby the Church at that time was being turned into a house of darkness and confusion. But by this statement God was creating His own fissure of the ceiling, that the light of truth might seep through and enlighten us as to the state of affairs in Rome.

It is no secret, and is a well known and documented fact, that the agents of Communism began entering our Catholic seminaries as far back as the 30s for the purpose of destroying the Church from within. Over a thousand such agents had entered the seminaries prior to 1940. The testimonies of ex-communists like Bella Dodd and Manning Johnson who had testified before the House Un-American Activities Committee about their subversive activity more than confirm that these agents of the sickle and hammer had been building their forces against the Church with the intent of breaking in and re-indoctrinating the faithful with anti-church principles.

Their plan was to first absorb Catholic philosophy and teaching in the seminaries so as to give them inside access to masterfully communicate and pull the Catholic hierarchy away from their traditional roots, so that they in turn would embrace revolutionary ideas and become pawns of ecclesial subversion. The Leninist "clenched fist" ideal would now be applied in a spiritual way where the "empowerment of the laity" would be a means of overthrowing the Church's monarchical structure, so that a new sense of democracy and religious liberty would take precedence over the established rule of religion issuing from the Seat of Peter.

With this they would advance the pacifist delusion that *all* are forgiven and that a day of sunshine has dawned upon Christianity (New Pentecost). The objective here would be to [15] sedate the Church by erasing from our minds any notion of punishment or divine justice so that Catholics throughout the world would not be ready when the red forces suddenly made their move to invade the west.

15　*This directly coincides with the Soviet propaganda that was advanced in the early 90s that Communism had collapsed and was no longer a threat. This pacifist brainwashing has especially been applied to the Catholic Church since the Church is the main instrument on earth to strengthen the west against the errors of Communism through the propagation of apostolic truth issuing from the Chair of Peter. For this reason the papacy has always been the number-one enemy of the Communists, which was providentially foreshadowed by the fact that the Bolshevik revolution occurred in St. Petersburg Russia, bearing the name of the first pope, Peter.*

This anti-church movement, however, was basically in incubation prior to Vatican II. Though the agents of Communism had successfully infiltrated the seminaries and had become priests and bishops in the 50s, their activity was greatly restricted because of legitimate rules and regulations that were in force, and because the Communist world had not as yet been provided with a forum to present their radical ideas to the Church. We might say that the lock was on the gate, but that lock was removed when they opened up the Second Vatican Council on October 11, 1962. This was the major "fissure" through which satan entered the Church.

Right from the *Red* Horse's Mouth

There can be no denying the fact that the radical reforms of today were secretly fueled by Communist agents that had infiltrated the Council. The plans of one such agent to destroy the Church were published in a book by a Catholic nurse, Marie Carré, after she discovered the agent's memoirs in his briefcase while caring for him following an auto accident he had been in. Unfortunately he died shortly thereupon without being able to reveal his identity, so that he is known only by a code name that was assigned to him by the Soviet Secret Police, that being SS 1025. There were 1024 such agents that had gone before him, some of whom became bishops and who could have even penetrated to high positions within the Vatican. The agent's memoirs reveal how he had become a priest who later collaborated with progressives at Vatican II for the purpose of indoctrinating the Council with evil. The following is taken from his memoirs and is slightly edited to keep it concise. Parenthesized notes have been added by the editor to clarify the points made.

"We must put it into their heads, and especially priests, that the time has come to seek and work for the merging of all religions. We must, in particular, promote among Catholics a feeling of guilt concerning the 'ONE TRUTH' which they claim they alone possess. We must convince them that this attitude is a monstrous sin of pride, and that they must now seek reconciliation with other religions. This thought must be made to grow and be uppermost in their minds....

"I was fully confident now that I would eventually enter the seminary, and I was already making plans for the future especially as regards my work for the [Communist] Party. I was to inject into Catholic thinking a whole set of new values and a new train of thought. I was to foster remorse in their hearts, a gnawing sense of guilt, quoting the Gospel: *'Be One as the Father and I are One.'* That sense of guilt must grow into an obsession to the point of rehabilitating Martin Luther. They will be made to believe that schisms and heresies were caused by their own intransigence, that the time had come for them to atone and make reparation by throwing their arms open to their Protestant brethren and confessing their own sin of pride and stubbornness....

"We shall speak of man, stress his dignity and nobility. We must transform the language and thinking pattern of every Catholic. We must foster the mystique of the human race. At first, we shall say that God exists, but we shall point out that God remains forever outside the field of human experience, and experience is what counts for sensate beings (the environment). We shall lay much stress on experience and sensory perceptions. The positive, the experimental and the sensorial must be the basis of the new thinking. We shall say that, since God is invisible, the best way to serve Him is to set up a universal church in which all men can meet as brothers in mutual good-will, love, and understanding. This new mystique must finally obfuscate the concept of God of whom we shall speak less and less, except for saying that <u>we</u> are God because God is in everyone of us (e.g. "<u>we</u> are" the Body of Christ). In this manner, we shall re-direct the religious yearnings and superstitions of the people. We shall deify Man.

"Once Catholics have accepted this new mystique, we shall tell them to strip their churches bare of statues and ornaments because these things are unessential and abhorrent to their dear Protestant and Jewish brethren. Thus all symbols of Catholic worship and devotion will go by the board, and when they are gone devotions will go too. Yes, we shall promote an iconoclastic zeal especially among the younger generation. They themselves will destroy that jumble of statues, pictures, vestments, reliquaries, organs, etc. It would be a good idea, too, to spread a 'prophecy' that says: 'You shall see married priests, and you shall hear the Mass in the language of the people.' This should make our task easier. We shall incite women to assert their right to the priesthood....

"Once in Rome I met a priest-professor who was in our network. He was a scholar and a scriptural expert (Note: Bugnini was a scholar and professor).... The professor was already working on a draft for a New Order of the Mass, and he urged me to do likewise because, he said, it was greatly desirable that we should give the people different kinds of Masses; this will help destroy unity, the mainstay of Catholic power....

"In the Mass, the words "Real Presence" and "Transubstantiation" must be deleted. We shall speak of 'Meal' and 'Eucharist' instead. We shall destroy the Offertory and play down the Consecration and, at the same time, we shall stress the part played by the people. In the Mass, as it is today, the priest turns his back to the people and fills a sacrificial function which is intolerable. He appears to offer his Mass to the great Crucifix hanging over the ornate altar.

"We shall pull down the Crucifix, substitute a table for the altar, and turn it around so that the priest may assume a presidential function. The priest will speak to the people much more than before. In this manner the Mass will gradually cease to be regarded as an act of adoration to God, and will become a gathering and an act of human brotherhood. All these points will have to be elaborated in great detail and they may take anywhere up to 30 years before they are implemented, but I think that all my objectives will be fulfilled by 1974."

In the early 60s he said: "Thus I labored for twenty long years. Pius XII died in 1958. When John XXIII announced a new council, my interest was greatly stimulated. I reported to my chiefs (in Moscow) that this was perhaps the last battle: no effort should be spared. They were obviously of the same opinion because they immediately appointed me to the highest position in the West European network, and they gave me unlimited financial backing through our bank in Switzerland.

"Hearing that Pope John had appointed a commission to draw the schemas for the forthcoming Council, I immediately started to work on counter-schemas with the help of avant-garde theologians (Rhine fathers) who had been won over to our way of thinking. Thanks to my contacts I managed to obtain copies of the projected papal schemas: they were terrible! I was in a cold sweat! If these schemas are carried, my work of 20 years will have been in vain. I hastily put the finishing touch to my counter-schemas, and I circulated them. Eventually, they were tabled at the Council. Thanks to the cooperation of some bishops whose thinking had been conditioned previously, the majority of bishops, reactionary but ill-prepared, were completely disconcerted by the highly efficient and coherent interventions of our friends; most of my counter-schemas were carried....

"But I am not satisfied: many of my schemas, although they were accepted, **have been watered down by Pope Paul himself in contempt of the majority vote at the Council.** Fortunately, the revised versions contain many ambiguities; in this manner, it will be possible to initiate further changes, alleging that they are in the spirit of the Council.

"However, we must begin to work for Vatican III even now. Vatican III, as I see it, will mean the destruction of the Church and the death of God. Then, I shall come forward, not to nail Christ upon His Cross, but God Himself into His coffin." (Marie Carré, *AA 1025, Memoirs of an Anti-Apostle,* 1972)

The agent's participation at Vatican II is significant. We see that before the Council he was busy at work drafting up counter-schemas in competition with the papal schemas being prepared, and that these counter-schemas were presented and accepted at Vatican II. But we also see how Pope Paul himself came along and watered down the counter-schemas in contempt of the favor shown to them by the Council majority, and how the agent in turn beefed them back up by introducing more subtleties and ambiguities to insure that the Council would endorse them.

Clearly the pope was treading amidst treachery and deception, especially since many of the cardinals were consenting to this "collegial" agenda to compete with him. In all their slumber the cardinals never dreamed that the enemy had invaded the Council, but they were dreaming for thinking that these new proposals and innovations were part of the ongoing work of God to guide His Church. Something wasn't right, something didn't click. Something had gotten into the mix to distort doctrine and confuse Catholics about the Faith, and that something was the devil who, with his agents, had invaded the Church through "some fissure."

Paul VI is the only pope to date that has correctly identified the problem about the post-conciliar crisis. He sounded the alarm about the devil in the Church, but somehow the Church through this same influence has missed the obvious, as it continues to update and merge with other faiths under the illusion of divine guidance.

The Year of Faith is an appropriate time to take a closer look at this conciliar fissure, that we might observe more clearly how it was an opening for this sinister thread to weave itself into the Church's fabric and cloak the Mystical Body with a new garb.

Pope Paul vs. Bugnini

To get a clearer idea of Pope Paul's battles with the Vatican confederacy, it's good to focus again on Annibale Bugnini, since he was the central figure of the liturgical reform that stirred up so much controversy and marred Pope Paul's reputation. Unfortunately his academic credits made him all the more dangerous, since it gave credibility to his reform which in 1974, he proclaimed to be "a major conquest of the Catholic Church."

Bugnini's work as a liturgist goes back to 1947 when he began a twenty-year period as the director of "Ephemerides Liturgicae," one of Italy's best-known liturgical publications. He contributed to numerous scholarly publications, wrote articles on the liturgy for various encyclopedias and dictionaries and had a number of books published on the subject. But there was a hidden agenda at work from the beginning that slowly began to reveal his perditious tracks.

As a little example of Bugnini's deceptive workings in the Vatican, we cite you this little anecdote from 1974. The Consilium for the Reform of the Liturgy had in its ranks a number of liturgists including a Father Louis Bouyer who was opposed to the changes in the Mass. Bugnini argued his cause with Father Bouyer by telling him that Pope Paul VI wanted the new changes in the

Mass, and then Bugnini told Pope Paul that Bouyer and the "Consilium experts" had decided in favor of these changes. Obviously it was Bugnini who wanted the changes, and Pope Paul later acknowledged to Fr. Bouyer that Bugnini had deceived both of them. The following is an interview that took place between Pope Paul VI and Fr. Bouyer in 1974.

(Father Louis Bouyer)
— *I wrote to the Holy Father, Pope Paul VI, to tender my resignation as member of the Commission charged with the Liturgical Reform. The Holy Father sent for me at once and the following conversation ensued:*

Paul VI: Father, you are an unquestionable and unquestioned authority by your deep knowledge of the Church's liturgy and Tradition, and a specialist in this field. I do not understand why you have sent me your resignation, whilst your presence, is more than precious, it is indispensable!

Father Bouyer: Most Holy Father, if I am a specialist in this field, I tell you very simply that I resign because I do not agree with the reforms you are imposing! Why do you take no notice of the remarks we send you, and why do you do the opposite?

Paul VI: But I don't understand: I'm not imposing anything. I have never imposed anything in this field. I have complete trust in your competence and your propositions. It is you who are sending me proposals. When Fr. Bugnini comes to see me, he says: "Here is what the experts are asking for." And as you are an expert in this matter, I accept your judgment.

Father Bouyer: When we have studied a question, and have chosen what we can propose to you, in conscience, Father Bugnini took our text, and, then said to us that, having consulted you: "The Holy Father wants you to introduce these changes into the liturgy." And since I don't agree with your propositions, because they break with the Tradition of the Church, then I tender my resignation.

Paul VI: But not at all, Father, believe me, Father Bugnini tells me exactly the contrary: I have never refused a single one of your proposals. Father Bugnini came to find me and said: "The experts of the Commission charged with the Liturgical Reform asked for this and that." And since I am not a liturgical specialist, I tell you again, I have always accepted your judgment. I never said that to Monsignor Bugnini. I was deceived. Father Bugnini deceived me and deceived you.

Father Bouyer: That is, my dear friends, how the liturgical reform was done!

(The original French version of this early 1970s conversation between Father Bouyer and Pope Paul VI was translated by Father Anthony Chadwick who found the original version at this website: http://www.leforumcatholique.org/message)

Bugnini's subversive designs were evident long before the Vatican II Council, for which reason he sometimes was suspected of conspiracy. As far back as 1944 he had asked a Monsignor Arrigo Pintonello to translate some texts on the renewal of liturgy that had been written in part by German Protestants. His protestant connection is highlighted in a sermon delivered by His Excellency Bishop Lazo of the Philippines on Ascension Thursday, 1998:

"I discovered the real reason for the illegal suppression of the Traditional Latin Mass. The ancient Mass was an obstacle to the introduction of Ecumenism. The Catholic Mass contained Catholic dogmas, which Protestants denied. To achieve unity with protestant sects, the Tridentine Latin Mass had to be scrapped, being replaced by the Novus Ordo Missae. The Novus Ordo Missae was a concoction of Monsignor Annibale Bugnini, a Freemason. Six protestant ministers helped Monsignor Bugnini in fabricating it. The innovators saw to it that no Catholic dogmas offensive to protestant ears were left in the prayers. They deleted all that expressed the Catholic dogmas fully and replaced them with very ambiguous, protestantizing, and heretical things."

In the March 19, 1965 issue of *L' Osservatore Romano*, Archbishop Bugnini said, "We must strip from our Catholic prayers and from the Catholic liturgy everything which can be the shadow of a stumbling-block for our separated brethren... the Protestants."

We can understand why Archbishop Lefebvre declared the following in his *Letter to Friends and Benefactors* in March of 1976: "Now, when we hear in Rome that he who was the heart and soul of the liturgical reform is a Freemason, we may think that he is not the only one. The veil covering the greatest deceit ever to have mystified the clergy and baffled the faithful is doubtless beginning to be torn asunder."

It suffices to say that Pope Paul was not the wolf, but was a lamb among the brethren, though he was a bit naive. One of his virtuous faults was his unwillingness to see the evil in his fellow man, which unfortunately permitted certain evil ones to carry on in Rome. The Holy Father on occasion had been briefed about Bugnini's affiliation with the Freemasons but he would hear none of it.

Masonic Connection

But in July of 1975 the pope was forced against his will to learn of Bugnini's affiliation with the Freemasons. Bugnini had attended a meeting of the Secretariat of State where he forgot his briefcase. A dossier obtained from Bugnini's briefcase was personally brought to Pope Paul VI by a reputable high cardinal (Ottaviani presumably) who had obtained it from a monsignor who had opened the briefcase to see who it belonged to. The dossier contained private instructions from the Masonic Grand Master in Italy to Bugnini which convinced Pope Paul beyond any shadow of a doubt that he was a Freemason. The following is part of what Pope Paul read from the dossier and is dated June 14, 1964:

"Dear Buan [Masonic code name of Bugnini]:

"We communicate the task appointed to you by the Council of Brothers, in accordance with the Grand Master and the Assistant Princes to the Throne. We oblige you to spread de-Christianization by confusing rites and languages and to set priests, bishops and cardinals against each other.

Linguistic and ritualistic babel means victory for us, since linguistic and ritualistic unity has been the strength of the Church.... Everything must happen within a decade."

This correspondence is taken from Andrea Tornielli's "Dossie Liturgia Una Babel Programada," that appeared in the June 1992 issue of 30 Days. It coincides with Tito Casini's blockbuster book of April 1976, *In the Smoke of Satan-Towards the Final Clash,* in which the author states: "The reform has been conducted by this Bugnini who has been unmasked at last; he is indeed what we long expected: a Freemason." Casini here was reporting on the 'dossier' incident of July 1975 that caused Bugnini to be expelled from the Vatican later that summer (see p. 54).

The following now is a letter from Bugnini to the Grand Master of the Lodge updating him on the progress of his secret mission. This is dated July 2, 1967.

"Incomparable Grand Master: The de-sacralization is rapidly taking place. Another Instruction was published, which took effect on June 29. We can already sing victory, because the vulgar language is sovereign in the whole liturgy, including the essential parts.... The greatest liberty was given to choose between the various formulas, to individual creativity, and to chaos! In short, with this document I believe to have spread the principle of maximum licentiousness, in accordance with your wishes.

"I fought hard against my enemies from the Congregation of the Rites, and I had to use all my astuteness so that the Pope would approve it. By luck, we found the support of friends and brothers in Universa Laus *[International Association for the Study of Liturgical Music]*, who are faithful. I thank you for the funds sent and am waiting to see you soon. I embrace you,

Your Brother Buan."

Traditionalist Catholic writer Michael Davies investigated the allegations against Bugnini and made contact with the priest who had discovered the dossier in Bugnini's briefcase and who had "this information placed in the hands of Pope Paul VI by a cardinal." The matter is discussed at some length in his book, *How the Liturgy Fell Apart: The Enigma of Archbishop Bugnini,* wherein he shows how the pope at this point was convinced of Bugnini's affiliation with the Masonic lodge.

The story about the briefcase also appeared in Piers Compton's 1981 book, *The Broken Cross: The Hidden Hand in the Vatican.* Therein he states that Bugnini's Masonic membership was recorded in "The Italian Register" on April 23, 1963, "and that his code name was Buan."

As a result of Pope Paul's shocking discovery, Bugnini was suddenly dismissed as the head of the Congregation of Divine Worship, whereupon the Congregation itself was dissolved and merged with a new Congregation for the Sacraments which Bugnini wasn't even permitted to join. This occurred in July, 1975. Thereupon a plan was in motion to send him into a sort of exile by making him "papal nuncio" of Iran, which was announced in the press shortly thereafter.

The Freemasons of course are a satanic secret society committed solely to destroying the Catholic Church. Their practice of witchcraft, murder, and devil worship is no secret, for which reason the Church has always forbidden any association with them. Those who join them are accursed.

But this was the heat that Paul VI was working under during those turbulent years. He truly was a man of sorrows, seeing that many of his trusted ones were using their rank to misrepresent the Church before the world. In addition to their efforts to block his declaration on Mariology and Papal Primacy at Vatican II, there was also a move at the Council to cast aside the dogma of Papal Infallibility, to dump the "Syllabus of Errors" by Pius IX, and to forsake the Church's 2000-year claim to be the One True Church established by Christ, all of which was a vexation to him.

Also there was talk circulating in favor of birth control, which grieved the pope and prompted his valiant rebuttal which came to a triumphant fulfillment on July 25, 1968, when he issued "Humanae Vitae," forbidding any form of artificial contraception. This extraordinary encyclical is historic for the universal impact it has had in the saving of lives and souls, being the inspired work of God, and has been the very foundation of the Catholic pro-life movement of these last times. How is it that there are conservative Catholics who will not recognize the enormous good he did for the advance of traditional family values?

It is true that the pope sought dialogue with other peoples and religions including atheists and Communists, but this outreach proceeded from the purest charity to extend the riches of God to all peoples regardless of race, color, or creed. He earnestly desired the friendship of God to rest upon every human on earth and was never seeking to apologize for the Faith or to adopt their errors into the Church, as did the liberal bishops of the Council.

It was this Vatican confederacy that gave Pope Paul VI a bad name by constantly issuing statements and documents in his name which he had virtually nothing to do with. It is no secret that Cardinal Jean Villot, the Vatican Secretary of State from 1969 to 1979, had often forged his signature and sent out letters purporting to be from Pope Paul, or had issued directives as coming from the pope that were not from Paul VI.

For instance the pope on September 14, 1972, came down hard on the suggestion made that women might play a role in the priestly ministry with the distribution of sacraments. But on March 29, 1973, the Associated Press reported that "Pope Paul today ruled that women, regardless of whether they are nuns, may distribute Communion in Roman Catholic Churches." Or in May of 1969 the pope through his pastoral letter, "Memoriale Domini," denounced the practice of receiving Communion in the hand, stating that "the method on the tongue must be retained." Yet it wasn't long after this that "Pope Paul" had sanctioned Communion in the hand. With the Vatican's media connection being arranged through the Secretariat we saw many of Villot's designs being announced in Pope Paul's name. From 1972 on it was Villot and not Paul VI who called the shots in Rome. Villot's Masonic code names were listed as "Jeanni" and "Zurigo" in the July 1976 edition of *Bulletin De L' Occident Chrétien*.

Pope Paul and Cardinal Mindszenty

It is worth recounting the story surrounding the valiant shepherd, Cardinal Mindszenty of Hungary, who suffered imprisonment and torture in his home country for speaking out and defending his flock from the ravages of Communism that were intensifying after World War II. In 1956, as Communism tightened its grip on the Church in Hungary, Cardinal Mindszenty was given asylum at the American Embassy in Budapest where he languished for fifteen years, unable to leave the building, since the agents of Communism awaited him day and night to assassinate him should he leave the embassy.

But on September 28, 1971, the world heard that Cardinal Mindszenty had arrived in Rome at the invitation of Pope Paul VI. He was received with great joy and tenderness by the pope who embraced Cardinal Mindszenty and hung his own pectoral cross around his neck. They both concelebrated Mass and the Holy Father spoke of the Cardinal as **"a guest we have awaited with longing**... **a symbol of unshakeable strength rooted in faith and in selfless devotion to the Church."**

Again on October 23, 1971, Pope Paul VI concelebrated Mass with Cardinal Mindszenty. The pope gave Mindszenty his own cardinal's mantle and told him in Latin, **"You are and remain Archbishop of Esztergom and Primate of Hungary. Continue working and if you have difficulties, turn trustfully to us!"**

The Cardinal returned to his pastoral cares in the world, but on February 5, 1974, he received a shocking letter from "Pope Paul" declaring his reign as Archbishop terminated and the See of Esztergom vacant! The Vatican then announced to the world that

Cardinal Mindszenty had "retired" to conceal the fact that they had "deposed" him. Mindszenty himself would later testify to this. His Memoirs end with these words: "This is how I arrived at complete and total exile." The pope of course had nothing to do with his exile.

Given the state of affairs in Rome, the story of Cardinal Mindszenty's removal should come as no surprise. The mutual friendship between Pope Paul and Mindszenty angered the Secretary of State since the Secretariat since 1972 had been committed to protecting the 1962 Moscow-Vatican Treaty which guarantees Vatican respect for Communism. The dismissal of Mindszenty as the Catholic Primate of Hungary came then as a punishment for his open and courageous stand against Communism. The same persecution he received from the Communists in Hungary during the 40s and 50s was now being executed through the channels of the Vatican hierarchy.

However, what Mindszenty suffered was relatively minor compared to what Pope Paul had to endure at the hands of these Vatican bureaucrats. The pope was being undermined on every side by those he trusted, with much of this betrayal coming from Bugnini and the liturgists. The following from Kenneth Wolfe's November 2009 article in the New York Times shows to what extent Bugnini was overrunning the papal office:

"Bugnini changed so many things that [Pope] John's successor, Paul VI, sometimes did not know the latest directives. The pope once questioned the vestments set out for him by his staff, saying they were the wrong color, only to be told he [Bugnini] had eliminated the week-long celebration of Pentecost and could not wear the corresponding red garment for Mass. The pope's master of ceremonies then witnessed Paul VI break down in tears."

It was the pope's meekness and dove-like simplicity that irritated the Vatican bureaucracy. In their estimation Pope Paul VI was a fuddy-duddy with no charisma who was preventing the floodgates of the Council from breaking forth. Things were not progressing as smoothly as they wanted because of his indifference to their progressive reform, which in 1972 he had identified as the work of the devil. The devil was using these neo-Pharisees as pawns to advance the internal destruction of the Church, with Pope Paul VI being the prime object of their attack.

According to the saintly Padre Pio who had paid high tribute to Paul VI, the Holy Father was being crucified by his own. According to Fr. Malachi Martin who was a brilliant Vatican insider, author of several books, and advisor to three popes, sodomy and satanic sacrifice had been practiced secretly in the Vatican since the time of the Council. According to German author, Theodore Kolberg, there was a double of Pope Paul VI reigning in the Vatican from the mid-seventies on.

The Deception of the Century

Perhaps the most revolutionary period of modern Church history, aside from Vatican II, was the early-mid seventies when the radical reforms and changes began shifting into high gear. It was during this time that rumors and allegations of foul play began circulating in Rome in the wake of increasing sacrileges throughout the Church that were being advanced in the name of "Pope Paul VI." Everything from guitar liturgy, to Charismatic escapades, to the new mushrooming fad of receiving Communion in the hand gave the appearance that an uncanny force had come along to spur the new changes.

In his 1981 book, *The Broken Cross: The Hidden Hand in the Vatican,* Piers Compton covers this matter and brings forth some interesting observations that match those of other whistle-blowers that were surfacing at that time. Therein he states:

"At length, stories emanating from Rome of sacrilege and abuses committed in church, with the approval of the Pope, became so startling, that groups of people in Europe and America decided to take action.

"This culminated with a Mr. Daniel Scallen of the *Marian Press in Georgetown*, Ontario, Canada, employing the Pinkerton Detective Agency in New York to investigate. One of the agency's detectives was sent, in 1973, to Rome, and he returned with a story that dwarfed all other speculations, however sensational.

Paul VI

Impostor

"He had determined that there were two Popes living in the Vatican, Paul VI and an impostor who had been made to resemble Montini with the aid of plastic surgery. Several such operations were necessary, and when colour photographs of the false Pope were sent to interested circles in Munich, where the imposture is still receiving concentrated study, there were certain noticeable differences in the two sets of features that could not be overcome.

"To point out the differences: Montini had clear blue eyes, large, and being long-sighted he only required glasses for near viewing. The impostor had green eyes, small, and he wore glasses with thick lenses on all occasions."

The photos of the two men indeed are convincing and baffling all in one. Montini's photographs reveal a small mole or birth-mark between the left eye and the left ear. This does not appear in photographs of the impostor, whose left eyebrow was nearer to the eye than was Montini's.

The differences between the nose and the ears in the two men are also held as strong evidence. Montini's nose was Roman, and protruding somewhat over his mouth, while the impostor's nose, part straight and part hooked, was shorter. Those who subjected the photographs to professional examination claim to have detected the insertion of a plastic strip in the nose to make it appear more straight.

The above are standard news photos of the two men as they were seen and known in the press as Pope Paul VI. Note the visible difference in the nose. Pope Paul VI (left) has a longer, straighter, more pointed nose, while the impostor (right) has a shorter and rounder nose. The photos were taken only four years apart, Pope Paul in 1973 (left) and the impostor in 1977 (right). Trick photography was not used in either photograph. The photos speak for themselves and bear witness to the truth. The four years that lapsed between the two photos would not account for such a drastic difference in appearance.

The existence of an impostor pope in the Vatican during the seventies was no secret among political circles in Rome, and is well documented in Theodore Kolberg's 1977 release, *Der Betrug des Jahrhunderts (The Deception of the Century)*. Therein he substantiates his claim with numerous photos of the two popes, which show there was a double of Paul VI reigning in the Vatican from about 1974 on. From what we gather he was an Italian actor of great talent with the initials P.A.R., serving as a puppet under the control of those who had seized control of the Curia in 1972, namely, Cardinals Villot and Benelli, and Cardinal Casaroli, known also for his notorious KGB connections. As we understand it, they drugged the true pope and created this impostor, using the best of plastic surgeons, so that the true pope made very few appearances from that point on.

The reign of an impostor pope would explain the many discrepancies that had confused faithful Catholics concerning Pope Paul VI, for instance why he would denounce Communion in the hand in May of 1969, and why he would sanction it from 1975 on, or why he would condemn the Charismatic Movement in 1969, and why he would praise it in 1975. Having an impostor in Rome made it easier for modernists to get on with *their* reform, which up to that point had been hampered by the Holy Father's resistance.

To get a closer look at this Jekyll and Hyde effect, let us compare Pope Paul VI speaking on the Charismatic Movement in 1969 and 1972, and then again in 1975.

In May 1969, Pope Paul publicly denounced "the illusion of a free and charismatic Christianity" which "does not build, but demolishes," and deplored those who "have recourse to gratuitous charismatic suppositions in order to fill up the interior emptiness created by their own loss of confidence in the guidance of the Church."

Again he said: "Many who speak about the Church today say they are inspired by a prophetic spirit, and they appeal to the Holy Spirit as if the Divine Paraclete were at their disposal at all times. May God grant that this presumption, of elevating a personal experience into a criterion of religious doctrine, may not cause havoc!"

On May 17, 1972, Pope Paul VI also denounced the Charismatic Movement, saying that it attacks directly "the very existence of the Church," leading to "extinguishing the real flame of Pentecost, disregarding the thought of Christ and of the whole of Tradition."

Note that his words are clear, direct, and in line with the Spirit of Truth, the Holy Spirit. His point was to say that the Charismatic Movement has no connection with the Holy Spirit, and that we therefore should have no connection with it.

Now compare to the ambiguous mish-mash in which "Pope Paul" expresses praise for the Charismatic Movement at the Second International Renewal Conference in Rome on May 19, 1975:

[16] "How then could this 'spiritual renewal' not be 'a chance' for the church and for the world? And how, in this case, could one not take all the means to ensure that it remains so?... Nothing is more necessary for such a world, more and more secularized, than the testimony of this 'spiritual renewal', which we see the Holy Spirit bring about today in the most diverse regions and environments. Its manifestations are varied... in which each one, expressing himself freely, helps, supports and nourishes the prayer of others,

---

[16]   *From the Pinkerton report, it appears that the impostor was in Rome as early as 1973 so that there were actually two "popes" functioning in the Vatican from 1973 to 1975. The impostor apparently was the one addressing the Charismatic Conference in May 1975 since his praise of the Charismatics coupled with his sloppy delivery radically differ from the crystal clear doctrine and expression of the first two denunciations made by Pope Paul in 1969 and 1972. The drugging of the true pope occurred around summer of 1975, from which point there was virtually only one "pope" appearing in public.*

and, at the basis of everything, a personal conviction. This conviction has its source not only in instruction received by faith but also in a certain experience of real life."

Note the emphasis on "personal conviction" which he says is born not only of the Faith, but of experience with the secular world. In other words, listen to the world and do what you want.

Pope Paul VI   Impostor

Voice Prints—Same exact Words
Different Voice Signatures

2a

pe cca t o r u m v e st r o r u m

Voice of "the Pope" on Easter, 1975

("the Pope" is Pope Paul VI)

2b

pe cca t o r u m v e st r o r u m

Voice of "the Pope" on Christmas, 1975

("the Pope" is the Imposter)

In his *Umsturz im Vatikan? (An Overthrow in the Vatican?)*, Kolberg presents further evidence for the existence of an impostor pope. Voice recordings of the pope's "Urbi et Orbi" speech were made on two different occasions, namely, Easter and Christmas 1975, with each recording containing the traditional Latin blessing, *Indulgentium Peccatorum.* The two recordings were submitted to Kay Elemetrics of Pine Brook, New Jersey, and passed through a voice-frequency analyzer. The output Type B/65 sonogram voice-prints of the same words pronounced by the "the Pope" on two different occasions revealed that it was two different men speaking on the recordings. Piers Compton comments in his book.

"It appeared, according to sonograms that were made – and sonograms are more sensitive than the ear – that the man who had spoken at Easter, and again at Christmas, had not been one and the same. There had been two different speakers. Here I quote from those who are qualified to judge the sonograms and sum up the distinctions:

"One voice had a much lower pitch than the other, with a more pronounced dragging of word syllables.

"Another difference was that one voice had a much lower range of frequencies. It emitted a more hissing sound, and was noticeably shaky."

Compton goes on to say: "The voice-prints were also submitted to the FBI for examination, and the same conclusions were arrived at. The voice patterns were different, and indicated that the vocal chords, the mouth, and the lips, were unique to each individual."

It should be pointed out that voice-prints, like finger prints or medical records, are valid evidence that hold up in a court of law.

An interesting point brought out in Compton's book is that it was the impostor who died at Castelgandolfo in Rome on August 6, 1978. A German bishop, who claimed to have proof that Montini was last known to be living outside the Vatican in the outskirts of Rome, had hoped to make this public in a forthcoming book. Compton also states the following in his book:

"A layman in search of more concrete evidence went to Brescia [Italy], where some of Montini's relations were living. There a niece informed him that they were perfectly well aware of the impostor, but that all their efforts to make it known had been stifled. The investigator, who was obviously untried and filled with a crusading zeal to bring things into the open, soon landed in trouble. He was jailed for four years, and afterwards deported from Italy. All efforts to trace his whereabouts since then have failed."

Another piece of evidence supporting the existence of an impostor was the observed difference of speech and behavior in the two men. From what we gather, dignitaries who had met with "Paul VI" in hopes of receiving some light and blessing were left perplexed and disappointed at his apparent inability to communicate, which was very much unlike Paul VI. Pope Paul was highly intelligent, cordial, and apt to communicate, so that there was virtually nothing on a spiritual, political, or sociological level that he couldn't answer with skill and command.

The impostor, though gifted as an actor, had only received an elementary education, and consequently was in no position to answer weighty questions with coherence. Reports say that he was sent to school to better acquaint himself with Catholic philosophy and doctrine.

His lack of formal training was evident when some European statesmen and nobles were granted private audiences with him in fall of 1975. When queries of depth were submitted his way, his responses took the shape of comments rather than answers, but which lacked the light and capacity characteristic of Pope Paul VI. From such occasions, it was unanimous to these statesmen and Church dignitaries that something was rotten in Rome.

For instance, the President of France, Valery Giscard d'Estaing, spent an hour attempting to discuss the prospect of developing backward lands in Lebanon as the groundwork for eventually attaining freedom of speech, to which the "pope" merely said: "I have found great faith and I am deeply impressed with it." When the French President was asked by a confused journalist if the man with whom he had spoken was really Paul VI, Valery Giscard sarcastically uttered in weary boredom: "But that is certainly absurd."

On another occasion in November of 1975, Gerhard Stoltenberg, Minister President of Schleswig-Holstein, was asked if he were convinced that the man he had spoken with was Paul VI, and Stoltenberg retorted in a semi-disgusted, semi-humorous tone: "That is certainly laughable."

It was from these and other like observations, coupled with audiovisual evidence, that dignitaries in Rome began circulating the word among themselves that there was an impostor pope in the Vatican. It is said that the impostor was first photographed on December 11, 1974.

The reign of the impostor would probably account for the fact that there were no papal encyclicals issued during this time, since the issuance of an encyclical would require the wisdom of a true pope. The pope's lesser writings (audience speeches, moto proprios, Apostolic letters) could have easily been forged by Villot and his aides, but an encyclical would be beyond their capacity. Pope Paul's last encyclical was "Humanae Vitae," issued July 25, 1968.

Switzerland Exorcisms

The following revelations are from a solemn exorcism that took place in Switzerland from 1975-1978 in which the demons under constraint were forced to reveal certain things about the Church. The session below is from April 25, 1977 and concerns Pope Paul VI and his double. Speaking through a possessed woman, the demons were forced by the Holy Virgin to tell the truth under the Solemn Church Exorcism, which was witnessed by several priests (see below) who all expressed their conviction of the authenticity of the revelations made by the fallen spirits by the order of the Blessed Virgin. The exorcisms are recorded in a book by Jean Marty (translated from French by Nancy Knowles Smith) entitled, *Avertissements de l'Au'dela a l'Eglise Contemporaine - Aveux de l'Eufer (Warnings From Beyond)*. The revelations have been edited slightly.

Exorcists:

Abbot Albertl`Arx, Niederbuchorten, Abbot Arnold Elig, Ramiswil, Abbot Ernest Fischer, Missionary, Gossau (St.Gall), Rev. Father Pius Gervasi, O.S.B., Disentis, Abbot Karl Holdener, Ried, Rev. Father Gregoire Meyer,—Trimbach, Rev. Father Robert Rinderer, C.P.P.S., Auw, Abbot Louis Veillard, CerneuxPequignot. (Two other French priests also participated in the exorcisms)

E = Exorcist

B = Beelzebub

E: In the name of Jesus, tell the truth, Beelzebub, in the name of the Precious Blood of Jesus Christ, speak!

B: She (the Blessed Virgin) makes me say: Alas! Alas! Some of the cardinals who surround the pope are wolves and...

E: Continue, in the name of Jesus, speak, Beelzebub!

B: We are doing everything to prevent people from becoming aware that there is a second Pope functioning. We are shrewder than all men put together. We are doing everything to keep that hidden... even "traditionalist" priests and lay people do not want to believe it nor to acknowledge it....

E: In the name of Jesus, speak only the truth!

B: For there reigns (in a loud voice) in actual fact, there reigns a false Pope, an imitation Pope. It is important that people are woken up gradually, for they are nearly all asleep.

Pope Paul VI (left) has a longer, more pointed nose compared to the Impostor (right) whose nose is shorter and rounder.

(Session of June 10, 1977)

E: Does Pope Paul VI know that he has a double?

B: At all events, he knows what is going on.... He is suffering unspeakably because, owing to what those cardinals are doing [forging false statements in his name], it is not what Heaven and what he himself would wish which is published in the world and in the Church, and which reaches the bishops. He is very well aware that he is like a prisoner, that he is, as it were, a prisoner of the Vatican. He suffers a great torment because of this.

E: Is the Pope informed about the cardinals? Has he investigated them? In the name of the Most Blessed Virgin Mother of God, tell us the truth!

B: ... He knows everything, everything, but he can do nothing. As we have said, his hands and feet are tied. He can do nothing, he receives injections. The doctor—listen carefully—who treats the Pope, is manipulated in such a way that <u>the Pope receives certain</u>

poisons which are harmful to his head and to his mind. But in spite of that, he knows perfectly well what is good.... His strength is always so paralyzed, so reduced, that he no longer has the power to stand alone against the others. That is his martyrdom. It is a heavy trial and is permitted from On High. He is, as we have said, a martyr Pope. He who does not believe this will see, his eyes will be opened.

E: How does one recognize the double?

B: We have already had to tell you that previously. Pick up the manuscripts, there is more about it in them than we wanted to say; single out the revelations in which we spoke about the double on earlier occasions, and then read Kolberg's book: "Conspiracy in the Vatican?"

E: Is what Kolberg wrote correct?

B: It is correct.

E: Has Kolberg written the truth? In his book, "Conspiracy in the Vatican?", is he telling the truth?

B: Kolberg tells the truth in his book. He has only a few small things that are not completely correct; but that is not very important.

Perhaps the most shocking and revealing information on the impostor is found in the prophetic revelations of the Blessed Virgin to the late seer, Veronica of the Cross of Bayside NY (1970-1995). Though the revelations still await investigation by Church officials, the message is widely circulated and is like no other of our time in providing the Church with penetrating insight into the current state of affairs in Rome. According to the message, the present day usurping of the papacy constitutes the essential point of the Third Secret of Fatima, which unfortunately was covered up in June 2000 after John Paul II had initiated a move to release the Secret.

We mentioned before how the dark forces had initially besieged and overtaken the Second Vatican Council, and how this plan was kicked into play in the first week of the Council when the vote needed to determine the members of the conciliar commissions was suddenly blocked, allowing radical progressives to capture a controlling number of seats on the Council. This historic takeover of Vatican II took place on October 13, 1962, the 45th Anniversary of the Virgin Mary's last apparition at Fatima. Consider the following from Jesus to Veronica, on June 18, 1986:

"On that date, as promised at Fatima, satan entered My Church upon earth. He brought with him his agents—and Satan himself, the deceiver of all mankind—sat in on Vatican II, and maneuvered all the outsiders to come in and distort My doctrines and distort the truth."

Changes not from Pope

Now in the message of September 27, 1975, it was stated: "You must go back in the immediate years and bring the knowledge to mankind that these changes, the changes that have given bad fruits have not been given to you through the Holy Spirit and through your Vicar, Pope Paul VI. It is the web of satan reaching out." In this same message, the Blessed Virgin went on to reveal the deception of the century.

"My child, I bring to you a sad truth, one that must be made known to mankind. In doing this, My child, you must proceed without fear. It must be made known to mankind. Our dear beloved Vicar, Pope Paul VI, he suffers much at the hands of those he trusts. My child, shout it from the rooftops. He is not able to do his mission. They have laid him low, My child. He is ill, he is very ill. Now there is one who is ruling in his place, an impostor, created from the minds of the agents of satan. Plastic surgery, My child—the best of surgeons were used to create this impostor. Shout from the rooftops! He must be exposed and removed.

"Behind him, My child, there are three who have given themselves to satan. You do not receive the truth in your country and the world. Your Vicar is a prisoner.

| Cardinal Casaroli | Cardinal Villot | Cardinal Benelli |

"Antonio Casaroli, you shall condemn your soul to hell! Giovanni Benelli, what road have you taken? You are on the road to hell and damnation! Villot, leader of evil, take yourself from among those traitors; you are not unknown to the Eternal Father. You consort with the synagogue of satan. Do you think you shall not pay for the destruction of souls in My Son's House?

"The Antichrist, the forces of evil, have gathered, My children, within the Eternal City. You must make it known to mankind that all that is coming from Rome is coming from darkness. The light has not passed that way. The appearance in public is not Paul VI, it is the impostor pope. Medication of evil has dulled the brain of the true Pope, Pope Paul VI. They send into his veins poison to dull his reasoning and paralyze his legs. What evil creature have you opened the doors to the Eternal City and admitted? The agents of satan! You plan to remove the Eternal Father from your heart and the hearts of those whom you seek to deceive. You scatter the flock.

"My children, you must now pray for the light. You must know the truth. All that is given to you is being sent from the traitorous heart of those who have seized power in the Eternal City of Rome."

In this same message of September 27, 1975, the Virgin also said: "It is the diabolical plan of satan to have the hate of the world turned to the Vicar, Pope Paul VI, in Rome. The plan of satan is to heap upon his shoulders all the error and wrongdoing; however, those whom he has trusted have betrayed him, have now assumed complete control of his mission. There are in figurative language, My child, [17] three popes now in Rome. Three popes, My child, not counting Pope Paul VI: three men who are being directed by satan. You cannot accept now what comes from Rome, for they do not come--these bulls and these directions are not written by the pen of Pope Paul VI. They are written by the pen of Benelli and Villot."

As early as 1971, the Bayside message warned that there was a plot against Pope Paul's life: "Your Vicar, your father on earth, will need your consolation. He is much grieved, My children, by the disobedience about him. There are many who are already plotting against his life." (September 14, 1971). Our Lady's message also mentioned a "well-founded plan" that had been devised against Pope Paul VI: "Continue your prayers and sacrifices for your Vicar. The enemy has a well-founded plan to remove him from the Seat of Peter." (April 1, 1972)

On August 14, 1976, this well-founded plan was discussed in more detail. "It is common knowledge now in the city of Rome that there is one who has been impersonating your Vicar, an actor of great talent; one who through surgery has gained the countenance of your Vicar. It is now common knowledge." (Our Lady, August 14, 1976)

---

[17] *Presumably Cardinals Casaroli, Benelli, and Villot acting as the three ring leaders in this monstrous takeover of the Vatican.*

In the message of March 18, 1977, it was also stated, "Yes, it is a fact and a truth that there is another who impersonates him and goes about having photographs taken. And there is a voice that comes out upon your air waves, a very good imitation of your Holy Father. It is all the master deception created by the evil forces that are seeking to destroy your Faith."

Regarding Villot mentioned earlier, there was also reference made to him on August 21, 1974, when She said, "V does much damage to the Holy Father by changing his correspondence. V rewrites his letters. V censors his mail." On September 27, 1975, She said, "You cannot accept now what comes from Rome, for they do not come--these bulls, and these directions--are not written by the pen of Pope Paul VI. They are written by the pen of Benelli and Villot."

If Pope Paul had been in praise of the reform, none of this would have ever happened. But as it stands, he on occasion would bewail the changes and point out their deplorable fruits. Consider his statement from 1970 about Vatican II: "In many areas the Council has not so far given us peace but rather stirred up troubles and problems that in no way serve to strengthen the Kingdom of God within the Church or within its souls." (Archbishop Lefebvre, *Open Letter to Confused Catholics,* 1986) Is it any wonder why they crucified him?

The impostor of course was not the architect of the new changes. He was only a salesman, a puppet on a string. The new changes were already set in place long before he made his appearance. Paul VI wasn't selling the reform as liberals had hoped, so they bumped him off and put their own man in, after which the new changes quickly accelerated. It was during his reign that the spiritual revolution flared up, especially with respect to the new practice of receiving Communion in the hand, the use of Eucharistic Ministers, and the false ecumenical thinking that we embrace all religions and be "healed of all division."

But skeptics contend that with the intellectual and technological advance of our time, the enemies of the Church would never be able to get away with something like this. But think again. There have been a number of anti-popes of the past who reigned during times of less spiritual darkness when there was less technology to assist their designs, yet their administrations were accepted by the people. So if this was the case during times of greater spiritual enlightenment when the enemy was less equipped, how much greater is the likelihood of something like this happening during these days of deep spiritual darkness when the devil has at his disposal all the state-of-the-art technology (plastic surgery, media propaganda) to deceive the public with?

Nay, the world today is satan's stomping ground with the Church being his major stronghold, fulfilling the prophecy of Our Lady at La Salette: "Rome will lose the Faith and will become the seat of Antichrist." (1846) We might say the temple today is "possessed" because of its many sins (Daniel 8:12). The Church in our time is degenerating under the illusion of progress, thus providing the devil with a perfect opportunity to get away with all manner of lunacy like the [18] Charismatic Renewal, homosexual priests, and yes, the impostor pope of the middle-late 70s.

What made the people so vulnerable to his deceits was his seduction and charm. He rang the ears of the modern church by telling everyone what they wanted to hear, especially his praise of women's equality, gay rights, free choice, the empowerment of the laity as a "common priesthood," and the pacifist preaching that the all merciful God unconditionally accepts us as we are.

---

[18] *A diabolical sect wherein the devil presents himself as the Holy Spirit for the purpose of luring Catholics away from the institutionalized Church. Though it operates today within the Church, it is actually a wing of the New Age Movement that has infiltrated the Church for the purpose of bringing about a new religion having no connection with the Holy Spirit (so-called renewal). The blabbing in tongues and foaming at the mouth are but a surface indication of its evil, as the real purpose of this cult is to undermine the priesthood so that the authority of the priest falls into the hands of the laity where we have a form of anarchy among the faithful (lay empowerment). The fruits of this anti-church movement are a falling away from the Church and an embrace of sin under the illusion of being forgiven.*

Remember, the devil is a deceiver. He doesn't come with his horns and claws, but presents himself as an angel of light with words of peace and reconciliation for all. Unfortunately the modern church fell prey to this because it didn't have God before its eyes anymore. And why? Because they took away the Old Mass and set up the Novus Ordo where the priest faces the people, thus diverting the attention away from God and placing the emphasis on the community of man.

Unfortunately many Catholics believe that it was Paul VI who devised and implemented the new changes with the view that the Church should keep up with the times. This belief was much confirmed by the misrepresentation of the impostor who gave the impression that "Pope Paul" was in praise of all the radical changes that were coming on strong in the early-mid seventies. His damage remains and will continue to remain until that time when the Church can finally arrive at the truth of what happened in Rome during those pivotal years. "The truth will make you free." (John 8: 32)

POPE PAUL WILL PROBABLY go down to be the most abused pope of history. The progressives had great hopes of using him to sell their changes to the church, but as it turns out, he seldom had anything good to say about the reform, and was often expressing regrets, lamentations, and misgivings, and saying things like "the Council has stirred up troubles and problems." He was downright glum and dejected over Vatican II and made no bones about calling it a failure, which is why the progressivist faction wanted him out.

But it seems that his action to remove Archbishop Bugnini from the Congregation of Divine Worship in July 1975 was the last straw that triggered retaliation. For it was only two months later that we learned that Paul VI had been drugged and replaced by an impostor. Given the timing, the drugging of the pope seems to have occurred around August of that year. The voice-prints cited earlier lend credence to this. The recordings of the "pope" giving the two blessings on Easter and Christmas 1975 revealed that it was one man giving the blessing on Easter [Pope Paul] and another giving the "blessing" on Christmas [impostor]. It is safe to assume then that the intense drugging of Pope Paul began around mid-summer of 1975.

We can only surmise that the pope's "medication" was administered through his physicians, since we know that doctors these days have no trouble using their profession for crime if they are paid. Seemingly the doctors were paid to keep him under medical observation.

But in spite of his sedation, the pope was still able to surface and make some appearances in his final years. According to the revelations from the Switzerland exorcisms, the pope in his drugged state knew what was happening with the impostor, and was suffering greatly from this.

The question is asked: why didn't he announce this to the Church? Answer: it was probably too difficult to do in his weakened state, and embarrassing. Who would believe it? The fear of scandal alone would prevent him from saying anything like this, not to mention the fear of being given an extra dose to keep him quiet.

But then he wasn't entirely quiet. On the 60th Anniversary of the last apparition at Fatima, he made a shocking statement to the world unlike anything ever said from the Chair of Peter, and one that described this very situation in Rome. The aging pope said:

"The tail of the devil is functioning in the disintegration of the Catholic World. The darkness of Satan has entered and spread throughout the Catholic Church even to its summit. Apostasy, the loss of the faith, is spreading throughout the world and into the highest levels within the Church." (October 13, 1977, the 60th Anniversary of Our Lady of Fatima)

Herein the pope was letting out an S.O.S. and giving us a first hand look into the state of affairs in Rome, stating that the devil himself was now operating at the highest levels in the Vatican and spreading his pestilent darkness throughout the Universal Church.

Something drastic had to prompt this, and that something was this conspiracy in Rome to overthrow the papacy and Faith, which is the essential point of the Fatima Third Secret. And how interesting to note that he said this on the 60th Anniversary of Fatima, as if he was letting on to the gist of the Secret.

In the Gospel, Christ said that the gates of hell would never prevail against his Church, but by telling us this He was saying there would be a battle ahead, a battle that would culminate in the last times when a great many would depart the true Faith. "For there shall be a time, when they will not endure sound doctrine; but... will heap to themselves teachers, having itching ears." (2 Timothy 4:3)

So we might understand that this anti-pope that momentarily usurped the Chair of Peter in the mid-seventies was but a precursor to the anti-pope of history that is coming. Like the impostor, he will appeal to the masses by telling everyone what they want to hear. He'll preach that an age of peace and reconciliation has dawned, and that it is time to put away the archaic Church of Rome with its "bigoted dogmas" so that we can finally be one with the environment in a spirit of global peace and harmony. He too will be a Charismatic speaking in forked tongues, and in the name of peace he will seek to unite the Catholic Church with the world, which of course Christ will never permit. "For when they shall say, peace and security; then shall sudden destruction come upon them, as the pains upon her that is with child, and they shall not escape." (1 Thessalonians 5: 3)

Today's ecumenical cries of peace and unity are nothing more than candy coated revolution. The Church since the Council has been in a state of spiritual revolt, but this will materialize fully when we see all-out revolution in the streets of Rome. This revolution is being generated by the Masonic element which is thoroughly entrenched today in Rome. The Masonic P.2 Lodge in Italy had accidently spilled the beans about their plans in the 70s which forced the Freemasons to publicly disassociate themselves with the lodge for fear of exposure. However the leaked information speaks for itself. Consider item no. 11 from their 34 guidelines issued in March 1962 for the destruction of the Catholic Church:

"Stop the practice of saying Mass before the Holy Eucharist in the tabernacle. Do not allow any tabernacles on the tables used for the Mass. Make the table look like a dinner table. Make it portable, to imply that it is not sacred, but could do double duty for anything, such as a conference table or for playing cards. Later, put at least one chair at this table. Make the priest sit in this after Communion to signify that he rests after his meal. Never let the priest kneel at Mass, nor genuflect—people don't kneel at meals."

The Masonic plan against the Church from the beginning has been to establish a new secular order or *Novus Ordo Seclorum,* and the reform of the Second Vatican Council laid the groundwork to start paving the way for this new order that would extol the doctrine of Antichrist, which teaches *peace and oneness with the environment,* as opposed to *peace and oneness with Jesus Crucified*, the true way taught by SS. Peter, John, Dominic, and Francis.

This conciliar vision for the unification of all religions was foreshadowed in the writings of nineteenth century Freemason and excommunicated priest, Canon Roca (1830-1893), who predicted that "the liturgy of the Roman Church will shortly undergo a transformation at an ecumenical council" in a move "to deprive the Church of its supernatural character, to amalgamate it with the world, to interweave the denominations ecumenically instead of letting them run side by side as separate confessions, and thus to pave the way for a standard world religion in the centralized world state." (His Excellency Rudolph Graber, *Athanasius and the Church in our Time,* 1974)

Many of the clerics and periti at Vatican II were Freemasons who subtly inscribed these ecumenical principles into its documents with the view that they would later serve as a handbook for the new conciliar church, especially the documents *Unitatis Redintegratio, Lumen Gentium, and Nostra Aetate,* that deal with Ecumenism.

But the people who penned these documents were the very people mentioned before who bullied their way into their conciliar high-seats and who opposed Paul VI on many issues, later causing him to make his statement about the "interior revolution" through which the Church was "attacking itself." Yet these purveyors of error conveniently placed his name on all the documents to sell their heresy to the Church, which is the punch-line of this discussion.

For the plan of the Freemasons at Vatican II wasn't only to generate the new reform, but to hide and shift the blame onto Pope Paul so that he would be seen as the author of all the problems. It calls to mind the French Revolution which was also generated by the Freemasons, who then laid low and blamed Marie Antoinette for all the problems, circulating lies that she was a spoiled brat in cahoots with the Austrians and who behaved like a tramp, when in fact she was an honorable Roman Catholic who revered God and said the Rosary, and who lived in simplicity and austerity with clarity of conscience. She constantly wept and prayed for her countrymen whom she called her children. Her last letter before her execution is indeed touching and shows her heartfelt concern for her people, many of whom were misled about her.

Pope Paul likewise prayed for his children in a spirit of meekness, bearing all the blame and complaint that was being heaped upon him, and offering it for the Church. It calls to mind the Sermon on the Mount, where Christ said, "Blessed are they that suffer persecution for justice' sake: for theirs is the Kingdom of Heaven. Blessed are you when they shall revile you, and persecute you, and speak all that is evil against you, untruly, for my sake. Be glad and rejoice, for your reward is very great in Heaven." (Mt. 5:10-12)

"All that will live godly in Christ Jesus, shall suffer persecution."
(2 Timothy 3:12)

"Heroic Virtues"

Pope Paul VI was a solemn and serene individual who was well acquainted with suffering, a providential marking that set him apart from others. He was born a victim soul and endured heavy bouts with illness in his youth that would often interrupt his education. His parents did not expect him to live beyond his first year.

But his bouts with suffering were an essential part of his formation that purified him from his early years and made him compassionable with others. This laid the groundwork for the ministry of the cross that he would embrace for the salvation of his fellow man, even unto that time when they would virtually put him on the cross.

In 1970 Archbishop Fulton Sheen had the opportunity to speak personally with Pope Paul VI, and he said to him, "You are well named," referencing how he took on the name of the persecuted Apostle Paul who went from city to city, and was stoned from Lystra to Derby, to Antioch to Pisidia. The Archbishop said, "You were stoned by your own." The pope replied, "Yes, I open my mail at midnight and in almost every letter is a thorn, and when I put my head on my pillow an hour or two later, I really lay it down upon a crown of thorns."

Continuing he said, "But I cannot tell you what ineffable joy I have to suffer." The pope then quoted him Colossians 1:24: "I now rejoice in my sufferings for you, and fill up those things that are wanting of the sufferings of Christ, in my flesh, for his body, which is the church." The Holy Father then said: "I suffer all of this for the sake of the Church."

Pope Paul's confessor, Fr. Paolo Dezza, gives us some insight into Paul VI who he always referred to as "a man of great joy." He said of the late pontiff: "If Paul VI was not a saint when he was elected Pope, he became one during his pontificate. I was able to witness not only with what energy and dedication he toiled for Christ and the Church but also and above all, how much he suffered for Christ and the Church. I always admired not only his deep inner resignation but also his constant abandonment to divine providence."

Yes, Pope Paul suffered in a constant labor of love to console and bear the pains of those who were disheartened and in need. He was a man of great fraternal charity who gave his life for the Church, and who went to great extent to answer correspondence during his secretaryship under Pius XII while still a cardinal. During the war years, thousands of letters from all parts of the world arrived at the pope's desk, most of them asking for prayer, help, and understanding, and Montini was given the task to formulate the replies in the name of Pius XII, expressing his empathy and understanding, and providing help where possible.

At the pope's request, he also created an information office for prisoners of war and refugees, which in the years of its existence from 1939 to 1947 received 9,891,497 information requests and produced over eleven million answers about missing persons. Even as pope he would later continue to receive and answer correspondence in a personal, heartfelt manner, where he took each soul personally and confidentially.

At the request of the Pope Pius XII, Montini together with three others also created the *Pontificia Commissione di Assistenza,* which aided large numbers of Romans and refugees from everywhere with shelter, food and other material aid. In Rome alone this organization distributed almost two million portions of free food just in the year 1944. The Vatican and the papal residence, Castel Gandolfo, were opened to refugees, and some 15,000 persons lived in Castel Gandolfo alone, supported by the Pontificia Commissione.

Also at the pope's request, Montini was involved in the reestablishment of Church asylum, providing protection to hundreds of Allied soldiers that had escaped from prison camps, namely, Jews, anti-Fascists and Socialists, and after the liberation of Rome, German soldiers, partisans and other displaced persons. Later as Pope, Montini would convert the Pontificia Commissione di Assistenza into Rome's leading charity organization, *Caritas Italiana,* which would later grow to international proportions with active service to the needy in 64 countries today.

In 1954 Pope Pius XII appointed Montini Archbishop of Milan, and presented the new Archbishop "as his personal gift to Milan." Thereupon Montini consecrated a hundred new churches with the belief that the House of God was the only habitation on earth that could serve as a refuge for the poor and broken hearted. Accordingly he sought to use Church monies to build or convert old church facilities into shelters for the poor and the homeless, a gesture that was looked down on by ecclesiastical bureaucrats and which partly contributed to his reputation as a "liberal." But in that sense, we're all called to be liberal; it's the most conservative thing a Catholic can do.

The foregoing is not to mention the tremendous charity and respect Montini had for the two popes he worked under while assigned at the Secretariat of State, they being Pius XI and Pius XII. He viewed Pius XI with awe, adopting the view that *learning is a life long process,* and after the election of Pius XII, Montini had the opportunity to meet the pope every morning until 1954, which enabled him to develop a rather close relationship with him. He was a keen observer, and his years of service under the pope provided an excellent pedagogue to prepare him for the office he would later fill. Consider his observation of Pope Pius:

"The goodness of Pope Pius XII opened to me the opportunity to look into the thoughts, even into the soul of this great pontiff. I could quote many details how Pius XII, always using measured and moderate speech, was hiding, nay revealing a noble position of great strength and fearless courage."

Montini's admiration was almost filial when describing the pope: "His richly cultivated mind, his unusual capacity for thought and study led him to avoid all distractions and every unnecessary relaxation. He wished to enter fully into the history of his own afflicted time: with a deep understanding, that he was himself a part of that history. He wished to participate fully in it, to share his sufferings in his own heart and soul."

Pope Pius XII indeed was saintly, which is why he was declared Venerable in 2009. When we think of him, we think of this heroic prince of the Church, this great pope of history, who reigned with such nobility and splendor, who shepherded the flock with such care and skill, never giving the least occasion to scandal, and who stood against the enemies of the Church while tending to the needs of the humble with unflinching courage. He truly was the "Angelic Shepherd" in [19] St. Malachy's vision, doing the work of charity under the Sun of Justice.

But who was his principal pawn for executing this charity but Cardinal Montini, who from 1944 on worked as Secretary of State for the internal affairs in the Vatican. Much of the correspondence addressed to the pope was passed on to him because of his charity and skill in communicating with people.

A closer look at Pope Paul's pastoral concerns gives us a clearer idea of who he was. While Archbishop of Milan, Montini went to great extent to expand the Church's pastoral ministry and used his authority to ensure that the designs of Pius XII were carried out at

---

[19]   *In 1139, St. Malachy received a vision in which he was shown all the popes from his day to the end of time. Each pope was given a symbolic name, which referred either to their place of birth, coat of arms, or some point about their pontificate. Of the 112 popes prophesied, the characteristic descriptions he gave match each of the popes with alarming accuracy. For instance the 107th pope of his vision, John XXIII, was called "Pastor and Mariner", which ties with his former episcopate as the Patriarch of Venice, which is a "mariners" town. The 109th pope, John Paul I, was called "Of the Half Moon", who became pope on August 26, 1978, when there was a "half moon." Similarly, the 108th pope, Paul VI, was called "Flower of Flowers", which can be tied to his coat of arms depicting three fleurs-de-lis (iris blossoms) which providentially symbolize his sweetness and benevolence of character.*

the local level by employing innovative methods to reach the people of Milan with the Gospel. Huge posters announced that 1000 voices would be speaking to them on the Catholic Faith from 10 to 24 of November, 1957. More than 500 priests along with many bishops and cardinals delivered some 7000 sermons during the period, not only in churches, but in factories, meeting halls, houses, courtyards, schools, offices, military barracks, hospitals, hotels and other places where people meet. His goal was to reintroduce the Faith to a city without much religion. "If only we can say Our Father and know what this means, then we would understand the Christian Faith," Montini said. He recognized that Western Europe had become mission country again and was doing everything in his power to re-Christianize Europe.

In 1957 Pius XII asked Archbishop Montini to Rome, where he gave the main presentation to the Second World Congress of Lay Apostolate. In his previous role as Pro-Secretary to the pope, he had worked assiduously to unify a worldwide organization of lay people from 58 nations, representing 42 national organizations. He presented them to Pius XII in Rome in 1951. The second meeting in 1957 gave Montini an opportunity to express the lay apostolate in more clear and down-to-earth terms: "Apostolate means love. We will love all, but especially those, who need help." Love in Montini's eyes was to bring the riches of the Faith upon the people for their edification and eternal happiness, as the saints of previous centuries had done.

Accordingly, he condemned the shameful indecency of the modern world that violates and tears down this fabric of love which, according to the pope, cannot exist outside the chaste observance of God's commandments. Consider this excerpt from his July 1968 statement on human life: "Everything therefore in the modern means of social communication which arouses men's base passions and encourages low moral standards, as well as every obscenity in the written word and every form of indecency on the stage and screen, should be condemned publicly and unanimously by all those who have at heart the advance of civilization and the safeguarding of the outstanding values of the human spirit."

In light of these and other untold things, it is no wonder that Benedict XVI cited the "heroic virtues" of Pope Paul VI as the grounds for declaring him Venerable. Even so, Paul VI is still maligned and spat upon, just as he was betrayed by many of his cardinals, in keeping with St. Paul's prophecy: "All that will live godly in Christ Jesus, shall suffer persecution." (2 Timothy 3:12) Against great opposition from his subjects, Pope Paul stood forth in the midst and upheld the dignity of marriage, and issued the greatest pro-life statement of all time which laid the groundwork for the international pro-life movement that would ensue.

Detraction

Even so, we hear the same old accusations over and over: "he invented a new Mass which uses the wrong language," which of course he didn't do. Yet some of these people resort to some pretty choice language themselves in describing their feelings about Pope Paul, calling him "heretic," Judas," "anti-pope," "Freemason," and so on.

And of course there is the sensationalist tabloid splash in *L'Espresso* about Pope Paul's "homosexual relations," which of course no one has ever witnessed. The whole thing comes off as Hollywood gossip; everything is a whisper, a rumor, a giggle, an innuendo, with half-baked reports to entice the unstable, but no beef. It calls to mind the two dirty old men who falsely accused Susanna in the Garden (Daniel 13). The irony being that these accusations are circulated by AWOL Catholics and professed homosexuals like journalist, Roger Peyrefitte, apparently indignant over Pope Paul's anti-gay, pro-life position, and who was out to smear a deceased man who cannot defend his reputation.

One individual in particular, Fr. Luigi Villa, has done much to fuel this detraction against Pope Paul through his book, *Paul VI Beatified*, in which he imagines himself to expose Paul VI as an Antichrist figure, something reminiscent of the old "Chick Publications" or "Tony Alamo" tracts where the pope was portrayed with sunglasses in a bathing suit. Fr. Villa, now deceased, was a member of the Sedevacantist sect which maintains there has existed no papacy or Church since 1958 outside a tiny handful of pope-bashers that are authorized to elect their own priests and popes. Coming from such an out-of-touch frame of reference, how is it that they could possibly produce anything beyond biased subjectivism?

Fr. Villa claimed that the late great Padre Pio commissioned him to expose Freemasonry, which may or may not be the case; we'll never really know. But what we do know is that St. Padre Pio never commissioned Fr. Villa to bash Pope Paul VI. Anyone who knows anything about Padre Pio will tell you that he respected and reverenced Paul VI and humbly submitted to his authority, as did other saintly figures like Sister Lucy of Fatima and Mother Teresa of Calcutta.

But Padre Pio also recognized the "heroic virtues" of Pope Paul, acknowledging that he was being betrayed by his own for the saintly work he did in authoring "Humanae Vitae." What follows is the last letter written by Padre Pio before his death which was published in the October 10, 1968 edition of *L'Osservatore Romano,* the official Vatican Newspaper. The letter is addressed to Pope Paul VI, and is dated September 12, 1968.

St. Padre Pio

Your Holiness,

Availing myself of Your Holiness' meeting with the Capuchin Fathers, I unite myself in spirit with my Brothers, and in a spirit of faith, love and obedience to the greatness of Him whom you represent on earth, offer my respectful homage to Your August Person, humbly kneeling at Your feet.

The Capuchin Order has always been among the first in their love, fidelity and reverence for the Holy See.

I pray the Lord that its members remain ever thus, continuing their tradition of seriousness and religious asceticism, evangelical poverty, faithful observance of the Rule and Constitutions, renewing themselves in vigorous living and deep interior spirit— always ready, at the least gesture from Your Holiness, to go forward at once to assist the Church in her needs.

I know that your heart is suffering much these days on account of the happenings in the Church, for peace in the world, for the great needs of its peoples; but above all, for the lack of obedience of some, even Catholics, to the high teaching that you, assisted by the Holy Spirit and in the name of God, are giving us. I offer you my prayers and daily sufferings as a small but sincere contribution on the part of the least of your sons in order that God may give you comfort with his Grace to follow the straight and painful way in the defense of eternal truth, which never changes with the passing of the years.

Also, in the name of my spiritual children and the Prayer Groups, I thank you for your clear and decisive words that you especially pronounced in the last encyclical "Humanae Vitae"; and I reaffirm my faith, my unconditional obedience to your illuminated directions.

May God grant victory to the truth, peace to his Church, tranquility to the world, health and prosperity to your Holiness so that, once these fleeting doubts are dissipated, the Kingdom of God may triumph in all hearts, guided by your apostolic work as Supreme Pastor of all Christianity.

Prostrate at your feet, I beg you to bless me in the company of my brothers in religion, my spiritual children, the Prayer Groups, my sick ones and also to bless all our good endeavors which we are trying to fulfill under your protection in the name of Jesus.

Your Holiness' most humble servant,

Padre Pio, Capuchin
San Giovanni Rotondo
12th September, 1968

Obviously the tribute paid to Pope Paul by the saintly Padre Pio is no match to the detraction of Fr. Luigi, who claimed to act in the name of Padre Pio. What is impressive is that Padre Pio was one of the greatest saints of history, a miracle worker with the gifts of prophecy, bi-location, and the reading of hearts, who knew all the secrets of a person without ever having met him; there was virtually nothing that one could hide from him. But especially, he was the mega-priest of God, the great stigmatist, who bore the wounds of Jesus Christ for over fifty years, and who was critical of what a priest should and should not be.

So if Padre Pio referred to Paul VI as "The Supreme Pastor of all Christianity" to whose "illuminated directions" he reaffirmed his "unconditional obedience," then it means that the Sedevacantist cult should follow suit and share his good regards for the late pope, and kindly cease from their murmuring.

Paul VI made some mistakes in his pontificate, granted, but they were not major ones. Like the popes before and after him, he too was remiss about releasing the Third Secret of Fatima, and could have been more on his guard against clerical salesmen who were trying to win him with false proposals of peace.

Perhaps the most scandalous of these was Cardinal Augustin Bea, the head of the *Secretariat for the Promotion of Christian Unity,* who labored to merge the Catholic Church with other world religions in defiance of the Church's dogma that there is no salvation outside the Catholic Church (extra ecclesiam nulla salus). The purpose of the Secretariat was to make contacts with other organizations and religions outside the Catholic Church and invite their representatives to the Second Vatican Council as "observers."

They indeed were invited, but not as observers. They attended as active participants that had a major hand in drafting up the conciliar documents on Ecumenism and Religious Liberty, something that Bea and other Church officials openly boasted of. Unfortunately this part of the plan wasn't initially shown to the pope, but was kept from him. Bea was a sweet-talker who made his perfidy sound like charity and was able to convince the pope that he supported his aspirations to reach outsiders with the Faith, when in fact he was just gaining his confidence for his own perfidious ends. This is why Pope Paul allowed Communists and outsiders to attend the Second Vatican Council, because he actually believed there was a program of Catholic indoctrination underway for these "guests." He sometimes was soft and easily misled by proposals that sounded good.

His longing to see the world united with Christ was in one sense his downfall, because it made him gullible to believe that this was what the ecumenical movement of the Council was all about, not realizing that the devil was playing his advantage with him. The vultures preyed on his goodness and used it to steal many blessings and grants that permitted them to carry on their ecumenical agenda with the stamp of the Church's Magisterium.

However, the unity of Christians aspired for by the pope was that of their ecclesial union, their conversion. He reminded the Council fathers that only a few years earlier Pope Pius XII had issued his encyclical, *Mystici Corporis,* defining the true membership of Christ's Mystical Body, the Church. He asked them not to create new dogmatic definitions, but to explain in simple words how the Catholic Church sees itself in relation to the world.

Of course they didn't heed this, but proceeded merrily with their interfaith program which the media gleefully covered and flashed across the earth in the name of Pope Paul VI. The internationalist cabal controlled the media even back then so that any missteps or indiscretions on the part of the Church were used as loopholes against her in their plan to discredit the Catholic religion.

We saw this with the resignation of Cardinal Ottaviani from the Church's central administration on June 8, 1968. Pope Paul VI accepted his resignation and appointed Cardinal Franjo Seper of Yugoslavia to take his place as Pro-Prefect for the Congregation for the Doctrine of the Faith. Seper was a fair pick who reiterated the Church's stand against euthanasia, abortion, and priestly ordination of women, but because he was from a Communist country, the Associated Press had a field day with it. The event was seen as "a major turning point" in that Ottaviani was being replaced "by a prelate from a Communist country" which "signified the move of the half-billion-member Church away from rigid conservatism toward new experiments in modernism and changing relations with Communist countries."

Needless to say, Pope Paul VI was not in cahoots with Marxists and traitors, nor was he the raving innovator who fabricated the new designs for the Catholic Church. He was actually uncreative and square, not crafty, but simple, direct, serene, and overflowing with charity even in his darkest moments, always praying for his enemies and turning the other cheek. If nothing else, he penned what may very well go down to be the most fruitful encyclical of all time, "Humanae Vitae," which indisputably was the handiwork of God. "By their fruits you shall know them." (Matthew 7: 20)

Miscellaneous Reflections

Paul VI did a great service to the Church on June 29, 1972, when he stated to the world that "the smoke of satan entered into the temple of God." This was said on the ninth anniversary of his Coronation, just when the infernal smoke was getting thick in Rome. It's worth repeating again the other part of his statement:

"We believed that after the Council would come a day of sunshine in the history of the Church. But instead there has come a day of clouds and storms, and of darkness, of searching, and uncertainties.... And how did this come about? We will confide to you the thought that may be, we ourselves admit in free discussion, that may be unfounded, and that is that there has been a power, an adversary power. Let us call him by his name: the devil.

"It is as if from some mysterious fissure, no, it is not mysterious, from some fissure the smoke of Satan entered the temple of God."

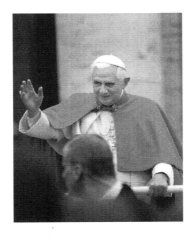

The pope deliberately worded his statement this way to identify the fissure as something that is no mystery, namely, the Council. Vatican II truly was the hatch through which the infernal enemy first slipped into the Church.

Now let us consider the words of Benedict XVI speaking on Vatican II. Pope Benedict, of course, was no fan of modernistic innovation, and he referred to the Mass of Vatican II as "fabricated liturgy" that had been snapped together in "a manufacturing process" to produce "a fabrication, a banal on-the-spot product." He knows, of course, who the real manufacturers of these pseudo-reforms were, and is well aware of the heroic martyrdom Paul VI suffered at their hands, having spent over fifty years in Rome as a brilliant Vatican insider.

Therefore he wasn't speaking idly in citing Pope Paul's "heroic virtues" as the criterion for his beatification. He knows of the illicit foul play that went on at the Council, and in his last days as pope he showed concern for disclosing some of this for the good of the Church. For the sake of exonerating Pope Paul, let us again diverge a bit by focusing on what Benedict XVI had to say about the real force that created the problems at Vatican Council II.

In his Audience with the Clergy of Rome on February 14, 2013, Pope Benedict spoke of the progressives at Vatican II "who sought the decentralization of the Church, power for the bishops and then, through the expression 'People of God', power for the people, the laity...popular sovereignty. Naturally, for them, this was the part to be approved, to be promulgated, to be favored."

This indeed was the agenda of reformers, to hand the power of the hierarchy to the laity for the empowerment of a "common priesthood" which would then serve to undermine the true priesthood. The new Mass was specifically designed to spearhead this socialist ideal, a point which Pope Benedict makes in his February 14 address:

"So too with the liturgy: there was no interest in liturgy as an act of faith, but as something where comprehensible things are done, a matter of community activity, something profane. And we know that there was a tendency, not without a certain historical basis, to say: sacrality is a pagan thing.... Sacrality must therefore be abolished, and profanity now spreads to worship: worship is no longer worship, but a community act, with communal participation: participation understood as activity. These translations, trivializations of the idea of the Council, were virulent in the process of putting the liturgical reform into practice."

Hence, Pope Benedict verifies what Traditionalist commentators have rightly maintained through the years, that the arch-rebels who held the reins at Vatican II were "virulent" in putting into practice a reform where the priest says a vernacular Mass facing the people and the people face each other in a spirit of communal festivity where the objective is "active participation" in busy-body fashion. This virulence was in force not only in the implementation but in the drafting of the Vatican II documents which centered around this novel theme of "active participation."

Clearly the draftsmen of this trivia did not mean that Catholics should be "active participants" in the Sacred Mysteries by their devout attendance at the Tridentine Mass. Nay, they meant what they meant, that "the rites are to be simplified" (Concilium 50), that traditional elements are to be "discarded" (50), that the main altar is to be turned around and moved "to permit walking around it and celebration facing the people" (Inter Oecumenici 91), that the Leonine Prayers are to be thrown out (Inter Oecumenini 48), and that cultural diversity should be brought in (Concilium 37) so that the people can be more actively involved with the community than with the sacred mysteries of the Faith. If the intent of these reformers was truly to see the Church more absorbed in the awesome and sacred mysteries of God, then they would have revered the traditional rites and would have never sought to "undertake with great care a general restoration of the liturgy" (Concilium 21). For the sacrosanct order of God needed no restoring in 1962!

To spur the promotion of the new reformed church, the liberal media played a major role at the Council with its biased coverage and carefully rehearsed applause lines to sell the new "aggiornamento" to the public. Pope Benedict exclamates this very point in his February 14 address:

"We know that this Council of the media was accessible to everyone. Therefore, this was the dominant one, the more effective one, and it created so many disasters, so many problems, so much suffering: seminaries closed, convents

closed, banal liturgy… and the real Council had difficulty establishing itself and taking shape; the virtual Council was stronger than the real Council."

The "virtual council" mentioned here was put together and orchestrated by that sinister "Rhine Alliance" that hijacked the opening session, discussed earlier. Of those living today who participated at Vatican II, Benedict XVI is perhaps the most qualified to comment on the Council, having attended it as one that was particularly perceptive and in the know. As with other qualified witnesses who participated, he knows full well what went on with the hijacking, as we will relate further below.

This rupture in the Church was not the fault of John XXIII, morally speaking, since he convoked the Second Vatican Council in 1962 to defend the Church against the errors of evolution and modernism, and initially had presented the Council with the 72 schemas that had sparked all the protest. Having read the Third Secret of Fatima he was alerted to the powers of darkness that were encroaching upon the Church, so he saw this as an opportunity to restate and uphold the Faith, though the calling of the Council was risky and naive. This is why Cardinal Montini said "this old boy does not know what a hornet's nest he is stirring up." But John XXIII meant well, as his objective was to use the Council to fight off the dark knights of secularism that were threatening the Church.

But when the doors of the Council were opened the storm of conspiracy rushed in beyond his wildest nightmares. We cited earlier the infamous coup d'etat through which his plan for the Council was blocked by the illicit interruption of the vote needed to elect the panel that would chair the drafting Commissions. Pope Benedict cites this historic incident in his February 14 address:

"On the programme for this first day were the elections of the Commissions, and lists of names had been prepared, in what was intended to be an impartial manner, and these lists were put to the vote. But right away the Fathers said: 'No, we do not simply want to vote for pre-prepared lists. *We* are the subject.' Then, it was necessary to postpone the elections, because the Fathers themselves wanted to begin to get to know each other, they wanted to prepare the lists themselves. <u>And so it was. Cardinal Liénart of Lille and Cardinal Frings of Cologne had said publicly: no, not this way. We want to make our own lists and elect our own candidates.</u>"

The above statement is of no small significance. Herein Benedict confesses that Lienart and his clique rejected the list of candidates that John XXIII had rightfully approved in an impartial manner, so that they in turn could create their own list and elect their own candidates. Conspiracy unveiled! According to the preeminent Romano Amerio who had contributed significantly to the drafting of the original Vatican II outline, the legal framework of the Council thereby was violated. "This departure from the original plan" came about "by an act breaking the Council's legal framework." (Professor Romano Amerio, *Iota Unum,* 1985)

The point being again, that Paul VI was not involved with this coup that gave birth to the "virtual council." Pope Paul alluded to this virtual council on the ninth anniversary of his Coronation when he said that the good efforts at Vatican II were hampered by "the devil" that came along "to suffocate the fruits of the Ecumenical Council." (June 29, 1972) That is to say, the virtual council won the contest at Vatican II, or as Benedict said, it was "stronger than the real Council."

If only the world had listened to Pope Paul's warning about satan in the Church! With all that has transpired in the past fifty years, it somehow hasn't dawned on the faithful that the ancient serpent reared its head at the Council and challenged the Faith to a dual. It was for reason that the Blessed Virgin at Fatima instructed Sr. Lucy have the Third Secret released by 1960, since it was only two years later that they would convene the Second Vatican Council, setting into motion an insidious departure from Tradition unmatched in the history of the Church.

The adversary's greatest victory came with the September 1964 conciliar instruction, *Inter Oecumenici,* article 48, which eliminated the traditional prayer to St. Michael after Mass, this being perhaps the most destructive reform of the Council. This was in keeping with the Concilium which states that "elements" which "were added with but little advantage are now to be discarded." [Article 50] The purpose of the 1964 document was to start implementing the norms of Vatican II as proposed, with the suppression of the St. Michael prayer being first on the agenda.

This was to prove fatal for the Church. For it was through the restraining force of this great Archangel that the influence of the devil was formerly held back through the ages and kept out of the Church (2 Thess. 2:6, 7). But by removing St. Michael this opened the door to infiltration and gave the enemy easy access to enter.

The timing of this move was certainly no accident, since it occurred just before the work to implement the New Mass had begun. The devil wanted the lock off the gate so he could get in there and remodel the fort without interference from his archrival, St. Michael. It was for reason that Pope Paul said that "one of the Church's greatest needs is to be defended against the evil we call the Devil." (General Audience, November 15, 1972)

The Holy Father's counsel is timely. For we see today a counter-reform in the works to rebuild the Church back to its true status of holiness as it stood before Vatican II. But if this plan of *true* restoration is to be effective, it must have at the center of its designs this counsel that St. Michael be again employed to guard the fort, so that it will offset the infernal one and procure the greater freedom and exaltation of Holy Mother, the Church.

In addition to invoking the protection of this Heavenly prince, we must also place this enterprise under the direction of Mary, *Mother of the Church.* For it is She who crushes the head of satan (Genesis 3:15), and it is She who has come forth in these latter times to lead this great battle against the forces of Antichrist that are waging their final assault against the Church.

Our Lady calls upon the true apostles of the last days to go forward with St. Michael as their guide, and restore the Church to its former glory. "For now is the time of all times, the end of all times." (La Salette, 1846) We are witnessing today the dawning of a great and glorious renewal for the Church as foretold in Holy Scripture: "At that time shall Michael rise up, the great prince, who standeth for the children of thy people." (Daniel 12:1)

Yes, it is time that the Church acknowledges that the removal of St. Michael at Vatican II is what widened that fissure for satan to enter. When Michael is returned, this will open the way to a glorious restoration which will usher in the *Era of Peace* promised by Our Lady at Fatima. The cause of St. Michael assumes more importance today than in any period of history since he is the guardian of the Faith whose mission is to lead the armies of God in the last times.

We pray that the cause of Michael be returned to the Church and that traditional discipline be restored so that the *Church Militant* can again be girt with that brilliance and armor "wherewith it may be able to extinguish all the fiery darts of the most wicked one." (Ephesians 6:16)

Humanae Vitae

With the process underway for the beatification of Pope Paul VI, it is appropriate to reflect briefly on his encyclical on the regulation of birth, "Humanae Vitae," as this will give us a closer look into the "heroic virtues" which Benedict XVI cites as the grounds for his canonization.

Pope Paul VI was truly a prophet of our time in the way he stood up before the world and declared that artificial contraception is a sin that ruins our relation with God and with one another. As Supreme Teacher of all Christianity, he made it very clear that contraception is forbidden and will never be accepted by the Catholic Church under any circumstances. His July 1968 encyclical on human life is a historic milestone which laid the foundation for the international pro-life movement of these latter times.

Consequently his action triggered hostile repercussions throughout the world, both within the Church and without. It brought upon him all the spittle and hatred of feminists who were addicted to their shameful promiscuity, as well as the scorn of our modernist high priests that were more committed to pacifying the shame of Eve than the injured heart of Christ.

But Pope Paul remained unmoved by the backlash he received from the modern world, because he expected it. He knew what he was getting into when he issued this, which made his action all the more admirable, since it showed the selfless dedication he had in doing what was best for his fellow man. He saw the verdict of divine justice coming upon humanity for its many crimes against life, and therefore was attempting to set some holy bulwarks into place that it might stem the tide of evil that was beginning to wash mankind out to *Death Sea*. Like the prophets of old he stood up on behalf of God and sounded a warning to the earth, stating that if God and his rule of law continued to be slighted there would follow divine repercussions in the very near future.

His prophecy was four-fold, and is unfolding in our time. Paul VI said that if society accepted contraception as a way of life, several consequences would inevitably result. First, contraception would lead to "conjugal infidelity and a general lowering of morality." This indeed has come to pass. The marital union that was created for the purpose of bringing children into the world has been reduced to a farce in many homes. Through artificial contraception, the Divine Founder of the marital institution has been blocked out so that decadent behavior has profaned many marriages, with lewd aberrations and even the practice of sodomy being condoned.

Hence the Sacrament of Marriage that was instituted for our sanctification has, for many couples, become an occasion of sin to separate them from God and advance their downfall. What the Archangel Raphael said in Holy Scripture directly applies to those who practice artificial birth control: "I will show thee who they are, over whom the devil can prevail. For they who in such manner receive matrimony, as to shut out God from themselves, and from their mind, and to give themselves to their lust, as the horse and mule, which hath not understanding, over them the devil hath power." (Tobias 6:17)

It is this very spirit of fornication that artificial birth control has fostered, as predicted by Paul VI, so that fornication (pre-marital and extra-marital) have skyrocketed in our time. And now the sins of the parents have been visited upon the children who think nothing of feasting their eyes on the despicable MTV channel and Internet porn. Being inflamed therewith, they're driven to go out and foul around with the aid of rock-music, Wicca, and drugs, so that the ubiquitous fire of sin burns out of control throughout our society.

But a major reason for this is because modern women insisted on taking their birth control pills in defiance of God's laws. Pope Paul said the pill would ignite the fire of sin so that there would ensue this "general lowering of morality." His prophecy has come to pass.

Secondly, Paul VI said that contraception would lead men to cease from respecting the honor of women which would cause them to treat women as "mere instruments of selfish enjoyment." In other words, the feminist pill would kill mutual love and promote the abuse of women. Clearly, his prophecy has been fulfilled many times over by pornography alone, which is the most lucrative business in the modern world. The entire industry is singularly dedicated to the abuse of women.

Thirdly, the Holy Father said that the widespread acceptance of contraception by couples would lead to a massive imposition of contraception by godless governments. He predicted that contraception would pass from a "lifestyle choice" to a weapon of mass destruction, which is being fulfilled in our time with Obamacare and government population control programs with their forced sterilization mandates. The pill is a deadly poison that has warped mankind's regard for life. Pregnancy today is treated like a disease that needs to be cured, so that under the whip of "big brother" abortion is now rampant throughout the earth with the annual abortion rate now at over 50,000,000. Don't expect Planned Parenthood to provide you with the correct figures.

Finally, the pope said that artificial contraception would lead man to feel that he can rule as a little god and exercise a limitless "domination over his own body and its functions." This hubris is perfectly expressed in such modern bio-tech horrors as vitro-fertilization, cloning, the creation of hybrid organisms, embryonic stem cell research, and the like.

The pill is largely to blame for these terrible evils in our modern world. It is a prolific seed that has helped society grow into the godless jungle it has become. It is a deadly poison that has helped to spawn this Apocalyptic culture of death that is now threatening the very life of mankind.

For the pill was a key part of the devil's strategy to start weakening the will of women by defiling their conscience and fostering disregard for life, thus paving the way for abortion through which satan would be strengthened and glorified on earth. For abortion is the negative current that charges the devil's battery and gives him power over mankind. This is why the murder of the unborn is so dear to him, because it gives him the needed power to bring about the fall of nations whereby they will soon be enslaved under the tyranny of a communistic one-world government. Pope Paul saw all of this coming, so as a good prophet he spoke the truth for God, that we "may have life, and may have it more abundantly." (John 10:10)

This truth issuing forth from the Chair of Peter must be adopted and echoed throughout the Churches of the world, especially by the clergy. If today's bishops and priests are truly interested in renewing their faith during the Year of Faith, then they must read and reread "Humanae Vitae" so that they will have that resolution and zeal to warn their people of contraception's destruction of the integrity of the marital act—as unitive and procreative—and how it has dire consequences for society and for souls. For it is truly a degrading poison that withers life and love both in marriage and in society.

In 2008 Fr. George Welzbacher, Professor at St. Thomas University, stated publicly: "The fruits of the contraceptive revolution point persuasively to the conclusion that Pope Paul VI was right and the world was wrong when he warned in Humanae Vitae that evil is evil and will bring forth evil, which 40 years later has come to pass." Amen to that! "By their fruits you shall know them." (Matthew 7:20)

None less than the saintly Padre Pio paid high tribute to Paul VI in his letter to His Holiness on September 12, 1968. Therein he pledged his unwavering allegiance to the pope in the face of demonic persecutions he was receiving because of Humanae Vitae. The late stigmatist said:

"I know that your heart is suffering much these days on account of the happenings in the Church, for peace in the world, for the great needs of its peoples; but above all, for the lack of obedience of some, even Catholics, to the high teaching that you, assisted by the Holy Spirit and in the name of God, are giving us.... In the name of my spiritual children and the Prayer Groups, I thank you for your clear and decisive words that you especially pronounced in the last encyclical "Humanae Vitae"; and I reaffirm my faith, my unconditional obedience to your illuminated directions." *(L'Osservatore Romano,* October 10, 1968)

Illuminated is right! In his letter St. Padre Pio acknowledged Paul VI as "The Supreme Teacher of all Christianity," and as such was the pope speaking ex-cathedra in declaring the essential point of his encyclical. It behooves us to focus on Article 14 where he declares:

"The direct interruption of the generative process already begun and, above all, all direct abortion, even for therapeutic reasons, are to be absolutely excluded as lawful means of regulating the number of children. Equally to be condemned, as the Magisterium of the Church has affirmed on many occasions, is direct sterilization, whether of the man or of the woman, whether permanent or temporary.

"Similarly excluded is any action which either before, at the moment of, or after sexual intercourse, is specifically intended to prevent procreation—whether as an end or as a means.

"Neither is it valid to argue, as a justification for sexual intercourse which is deliberately contraceptive, that a lesser evil is to be preferred to a greater one, or that such intercourse would merge with procreative acts of past and future to form a single entity, and so be qualified by exactly the same moral goodness as these. Though it is true that sometimes it is lawful to tolerate a lesser moral evil in order to avoid a greater evil or in order to promote a greater good," it is never lawful, even for the gravest reasons, to do evil that good may come of it—in other words, to intend directly something which of its very nature contradicts the moral order, and which must therefore be judged unworthy of man, even though the intention is to protect or promote the welfare of an individual, of a family or of society in general. Consequently, it is a serious error to think that a whole married life of otherwise normal relations can justify sexual intercourse which is deliberately contraceptive and so intrinsically wrong."

As a wholesome recourse for travailing couples that are not able to birth children at a given time, the pope benevolently recommends that they adopt the natural rhythm method of regulating birth. Even so, there are those who criticize this recommendation, arguing that it will encourage couples to deliberately duck-and-hide from God so that the [20] marital act is habitually used for non-procreative purposes. But this is not his design, and the good pope makes this very clear. The whole point of his encyclical is to say that God must be allowed to work through a couples' marriage, that He must be the very heart and center of this union whereby procreation is the end product and crowning achievement!

The rhythm method is only prescribed for couples who cannot make ends meet at a given time, or who for reasons of health or scandal decide they must defer the birthing of children to a later date. The pope is saying that they have this recourse to use the rhythm method for the purpose of preserving their union with God and with each other. He is pointing out that this is an acceptable path they should utilize for the preservation of their marital bond when the rearing of children is not in their immediate plans. The use of sex for unitive purposes only is always licit as long as couples are fully open to let God work through their union with no contraceptive obstructions thrown in the way.

---

[20]   *Couples should do a firm examination of conscience to make sure there are no selfish, feminist, or contraceptive motives behind their decision to use the rhythm method, lest they deceive themselves into thinking they are goody-good Catholics in observance of God's law, only to learn later in shock that their motives were no different than those promiscuous ones who lock God out of their marriage (Tobias 6:17).*

After all, older couples who are beyond the productive years are free to engage martially without offense, so how much more is this the case for younger couples in trying situations who need a wholesome recourse to preserve their grace with God.

The bottom line of "Humanae Vitae" is that artificial contraception is forbidden in the Christian life, which means that couples may never resort to the use of birth control pills, preventative or abortive, or to sterilization, or to surgical abortions of any kind. For such methods of regulating birth only ruin their relation with God and plague their marriage with guilt, leading to discord and divorce, and to their contribution to the growing culture of death on earth. Birth control feeds the infernal monster and gives him power over man, whereas the birthing and raising children is the victorious path that God has ordained for our salvation, especially that of the woman. St. Paul spells it out in clear, unambiguous terms: "She shall be saved through child bearing; if she continue in faith, and love, and sanctification, with sobriety." (1 Timothy 2: 15)

If even a sector of today's contraceptive women heeded Pope Paul's directive to renounce artificial birth control of every kind, it no doubt would stay the hand of execution that is poised to strike our world for its many executions against life. Faithful Catholics are encouraged to read Pope Paul's superlative encyclical on human life and to ponder his words well. For his prophecy is unfolding in our time.

ENCYCLICAL LETTER
HUMANAE VITAE
OF THE SUPREME PONTIFF
PAUL VI
TO HIS VENERABLE BROTHERS
THE PATRIARCHS, ARCHBISHOPS, BISHOPS
AND OTHER LOCAL ORDINARIES
IN PEACE AND COMMUNION WITH THE APOSTOLIC SEE,
TO THE CLERGY AND FAITHFUL OF THE WHOLE
CATHOLIC WORLD, AND TO ALL MEN OF GOOD WILL,
ON THE REGULATION OF BIRTH

Honored Brothers and Dear Sons, Health and Apostolic Benediction.

The transmission of human life is a most serious role in which married people collaborate freely and responsibly with God the Creator. It has always been a source of great joy to them, even though it sometimes entails many difficulties and hardships.

The fulfillment of this duty has always posed problems to the conscience of married people, but the recent course of human society and the concomitant changes have provoked new questions. The Church cannot ignore these questions, for they concern matters intimately connected with the life and happiness of human beings.

I.
PROBLEM AND COMPETENCY
OF THE MAGISTERIUM

2. The changes that have taken place are of considerable importance and varied in nature. In the first place there is the rapid increase in population which has made many fear that world population is going to grow faster than available resources, with the consequence that many families and developing countries would be faced with greater hardships. This can easily induce public authorities to be tempted to take even harsher measures to avert this danger. There is also the fact that not only working and housing conditions but the greater demands made both in the economic and educational field pose a living situation in which it is frequently difficult these days to provide properly for a large family.

Also noteworthy is a new understanding of the dignity of woman and her place in society, of the value of conjugal love in marriage and the relationship of conjugal acts to this love.

But the most remarkable development of all is to be seen in man's stupendous progress in the domination and rational organization of the forces of nature to the point that he is endeavoring to extend this control over every aspect of his own life—over his body, over his mind and emotions, over his social life, and even over the laws that regulate the transmission of life.

New Questions
3. This new state of things gives rise to new questions. Granted the conditions of life today and taking into account the relevance of married love to the harmony and mutual fidelity of husband and wife, would it not be right to review the moral norms in force till now, especially when it is felt that these can be observed only with the gravest difficulty, sometimes only by heroic effort?

Moreover, if one were to apply here the so called principle of totality, could it not be accepted that the intention to have a less prolific but more rationally planned family might transform an action which renders natural processes infertile into a licit and provident control of birth? Could it not be admitted, in other words, that procreative finality applies to the totality of married life rather than to each single act? A further question is whether, because people are more conscious today of their responsibilities, the time has not come when the transmission of life should be regulated by their intelligence and will rather than through the specific rhythms of their own bodies.

Interpreting the Moral Law

4. This kind of question requires from the teaching authority of the Church a new and deeper reflection on the principles of the moral teaching on marriage—a teaching which is based on the natural law as illuminated and enriched by divine Revelation.

No member of the faithful could possibly deny that the Church is competent in her Magisterium to interpret the natural moral law. It is in fact indisputable, as Our predecessors have many times declared, (I) that Jesus Christ, when He communicated His divine power to Peter and the other Apostles and sent them to teach all nations His commandments, (2) constituted them as the authentic guardians and interpreters of the whole moral law, not only, that is, of the law of the Gospel but also of the natural law. For the natural law, too, declares the will of God, and its faithful observance is necessary for men's eternal salvation. (3)

In carrying out this mandate, the Church has always issued appropriate documents on the nature of marriage, the correct use of conjugal rights, and the duties of spouses. These documents have been more copious in recent times. (4)

Special Studies

5. The consciousness of the same responsibility induced Us to confirm and expand the commission set up by Our predecessor Pope John XXIII, of happy memory, in March, 1963. This commission included married couples as well as many experts in the various fields pertinent to these questions. Its task was to examine views and opinions concerning married life, and especially on the correct regulation of births; and it was also to provide the teaching authority of the Church with such evidence as would enable it to give an apt reply in this matter, which not only the faithful but also the rest of the world were waiting for. (5)

When the evidence of the experts had been received, as well as the opinions and advice of a considerable number of Our brethren in the episcopate—some of whom sent their views spontaneously, while others were requested by Us to do so—We were in a position to weigh with more precision all the aspects of this complex subject. Hence We are deeply grateful to all those concerned.

The Magisterium's Reply

6. However, the conclusions arrived at by the commission could not be considered by Us as definitive and absolutely certain, dispensing Us from the duty of examining personally this serious question. This was all the more necessary because, within the commission itself, there was not complete agreement concerning the moral norms to be proposed, and especially because certain approaches and criteria for a solution to this question had emerged which were at variance with the moral doctrine on marriage constantly taught by the Magisterium of the Church.

Consequently, now that We have sifted carefully the evidence sent to Us and intently studied the whole matter, as well as prayed constantly to God, We, by virtue of the mandate entrusted to Us by Christ, intend to give Our reply to this series of grave questions.

II.
DOCTRINAL PRINCIPLES

7. The question of human procreation, like every other question which touches human life, involves more than the limited aspects specific to such disciplines as biology, psychology, demography or sociology. It is the whole man and the whole mission to which he is called that must be considered: both its natural, earthly aspects and its supernatural, eternal aspects. And since in the attempt to justify artificial methods of birth control many appeal to the demands of married love or of responsible parenthood, these two important realities of married life must be accurately defined and analyzed. This is what We mean to do, with special reference to what the Second Vatican Council taught with the highest authority in its Pastoral Constitution on the Church in the World of Today.

God's Loving Design

8. Married love particularly reveals its true nature and nobility when we realize that it takes its origin from God, who "is love," (6) the Father "from whom every family in heaven and on earth is named." (7)

Marriage, then, is far from being the effect of chance or the result of the blind evolution of natural forces. It is in reality the wise and provident institution of God the Creator, whose purpose was to effect in man His loving design. As a consequence, husband and wife, through that mutual gift of themselves, which is specific and exclusive to them alone, develop that union of two persons in which they perfect one another, cooperating with God in the generation and rearing of new lives.

The marriage of those who have been baptized is, in addition, invested with the dignity of a sacramental sign of grace, for it represents the union of Christ and His Church.

Married Love

9. In the light of these facts the characteristic features and exigencies of married love are clearly indicated, and it is of the highest importance to evaluate them exactly.

This love is above all fully human, a compound of sense and spirit. It is not, then, merely a question of natural instinct or emotional drive. It is also, and above all, an act of the free will, whose trust is such that it is meant not only to survive the joys and sorrows of daily life, but also to grow, so that husband and wife become in a way one heart and one soul, and together attain their human fulfillment.

It is a love which is total—that very special form of personal friendship in which husband and wife generously share everything, allowing no unreasonable exceptions and not thinking solely of their own convenience. Whoever really loves his partner loves not only for what he receives, but loves that partner for the partner's own sake, content to be able to enrich the other with the gift of himself.

Married love is also faithful and exclusive of all other, and this until death. This is how husband and wife understood it on the day on which, fully aware of what they were doing, they freely vowed themselves to one another in marriage. Though this fidelity of husband and wife sometimes presents difficulties, no one has the right to assert that it is impossible; it is, on the contrary, always honorable and meritorious. The example of countless married couples proves not only that fidelity is in accord with the nature of marriage, but also that it is the source of profound and enduring happiness.

Finally, this love is fecund. It is not confined wholly to the loving interchange of husband and wife; it also contrives to go beyond this to bring new life into being. "Marriage and conjugal love are by their nature ordained toward the procreation and education of children. Children are really the supreme gift of marriage and contribute in the highest degree to their parents' welfare." (8)

Responsible Parenthood
10. Married love, therefore, requires of husband and wife the full awareness of their obligations in the matter of responsible parenthood, which today, rightly enough, is much insisted upon, but which at the same time should be rightly understood. Thus, we do well to consider responsible parenthood in the light of its varied legitimate and interrelated aspects.

With regard to the biological processes, responsible parenthood means an awareness of, and respect for, their proper functions. In the procreative faculty the human mind discerns biological laws that apply to the human person. (9)

With regard to man's innate drives and emotions, responsible parenthood means that man's reason and will must exert control over them.

With regard to physical, economic, psychological and social conditions, responsible parenthood is exercised by those who prudently and generously decide to have more children, and by those who, for serious reasons and with due respect to moral precepts, decide not to have additional children for either a certain or an indefinite period of time.

Responsible parenthood, as we use the term here, has one further essential aspect of paramount importance. It concerns the objective moral order which was established by God, and of which a right conscience is the true interpreter. In a word, the exercise of responsible parenthood requires that husband and wife, keeping a right order of priorities, recognize their own duties toward God, themselves, their families and human society.

From this it follows that they are not free to act as they choose in the service of transmitting life, as if it were wholly up to them to decide what is the right course to follow. On the contrary, they are bound to ensure that what they do corresponds to the will of God the Creator. The very nature of marriage and its use makes His will clear, while the constant teaching of the Church spells it out. (10)

Observing the Natural Law

11. The sexual activity, in which husband and wife are intimately and chastely united with one another, through which human life is transmitted, is, as the recent Council recalled, "noble and worthy." (11) It does not, moreover, cease to be legitimate even when, for reasons independent of their will, it is foreseen to be infertile. For its natural adaptation to the expression and strengthening of the union of husband and wife is not thereby suppressed. The fact is, as experience shows, that new life is not the result of each and every act of sexual intercourse. God has wisely ordered laws of nature and the incidence of fertility in such a way that successive births are already naturally spaced through the inherent operation of these laws. The Church, nevertheless, in urging men to the observance of the precepts of the natural law, which it interprets by its constant doctrine, teaches that each and every marital act must of necessity retain its intrinsic relationship to the procreation of human life. (12)

Union and Procreation

12. This particular doctrine, often expounded by the Magisterium of the Church, is based on the inseparable connection, established by God, which man on his own initiative may not break, between the unitive significance and the procreative significance which are both inherent to the marriage act.

The reason is that the fundamental nature of the marriage act, while uniting husband and wife in the closest intimacy, also renders them capable of generating new life—and this as a result of laws written into the actual nature of man and of woman. And if each of these essential qualities, the unitive and the procreative, is preserved, the use of marriage fully retains its sense of true mutual love and its ordination to the supreme responsibility of parenthood to which man is called. We believe that our contemporaries are particularly capable of seeing that this teaching is in harmony with human reason.

Faithfulness to God's Design

13. Men rightly observe that a conjugal act imposed on one's partner without regard to his or her condition or personal and reasonable wishes in the matter, is no true act of love, and therefore offends the moral order in its particular application to the intimate relationship of husband and wife. If they further reflect, they must also recognize that an act of mutual love which impairs the capacity to transmit life which God the Creator, through specific laws, has built into it, frustrates His design which constitutes the norm of marriage, and contradicts the will of the Author of life. Hence to use this divine gift while depriving it, even if only partially, of its meaning and purpose, is equally repugnant to the nature of man and of woman, and is consequently in opposition to the plan of God and His holy will. But to experience the gift of married love while respecting the laws of conception is to acknowledge that one is not the master of the sources of life but rather the minister of the design established by the Creator. Just as man does not have unlimited dominion over his body in general, so also, and with more particular reason, he has no such dominion over his specifically sexual faculties, for these are concerned by their very nature with the generation of life, of which God is the source. "Human life is sacred—all men must recognize that fact," Our predecessor Pope John XXIII recalled. "From its very inception it reveals the creating hand of God." (13)

Unlawful Birth Control Methods
14. Therefore We base Our words on the first principles of a human and Christian doctrine of marriage when We are obliged once more to declare that the direct interruption of the generative process already begun and, above all, all direct abortion, even for therapeutic reasons, are to be absolutely excluded as lawful means of regulating the number of children. (14) Equally to be condemned, as the Magisterium of the Church has affirmed on many occasions, is direct sterilization, whether of the man or of the woman, whether permanent or temporary. (15)

Similarly excluded is any action which either before, at the moment of, or after sexual intercourse, is specifically intended to prevent procreation—whether as an end or as a means. (16)

Neither is it valid to argue, as a justification for sexual intercourse which is deliberately contraceptive, that a lesser evil is to be preferred to a greater one, or that such intercourse would merge with procreative acts of past and future to form a single entity, and so be qualified by exactly the same moral goodness as these. Though it is true that sometimes it is lawful to tolerate a lesser moral evil in order to avoid a greater evil or in order to promote a greater good," it is never lawful, even for the gravest reasons, to do evil that good may come of it (18)—in other words, to intend directly something which of its very nature contradicts the moral order, and which must therefore be judged unworthy of man, even though the intention is to protect or promote the welfare of an individual, of a family or of society in general. Consequently, it is a serious error to think that a whole married life of otherwise normal relations can justify sexual intercourse which is deliberately contraceptive and so intrinsically wrong.

Lawful Therapeutic Means

15. On the other hand, the Church does not consider at all illicit the use of those therapeutic means necessary to cure bodily diseases, even if a foreseeable impediment to procreation should result there from—provided such impediment is not directly intended for any motive whatsoever. (19)

Recourse to Infertile Periods

16. Now as We noted earlier (no. 3), some people today raise the objection against this particular doctrine of the Church concerning the moral laws governing marriage, that human intelligence has both the right and responsibility to control those forces of irrational nature which come within its ambit and to direct them toward ends beneficial to man. Others ask on the same point whether it is not reasonable in so many cases to use artificial birth control if by so doing the harmony and peace of a family are better served and more suitable conditions are provided for the education of children already born. To this question We must give a clear reply. The Church is the first to praise and commend the application of human intelligence to an activity in which a rational creature such as man is so closely associated with his Creator. But she affirms that this must be done within the limits of the order of reality established by God.

If therefore there are well-grounded reasons for spacing births, arising from the physical or psychological condition of husband or wife, or from external circumstances, the Church teaches that married people may then take advantage of the natural cycles immanent in the reproductive system and engage in marital intercourse only during those times that are infertile, thus controlling birth in a way which does not in the least offend the moral principles which We have just explained. (20)

Neither the Church nor her doctrine is inconsistent when she considers it lawful for married people to take advantage of the infertile period but condemns as always unlawful the use of means which directly prevent conception, even when the reasons given for the later practice may appear to be upright and serious. In reality, these two cases are completely different. In the former the married couple rightly use a faculty provided them by nature. In the later they obstruct the natural development of the generative process. It cannot be denied that in each case the married couple, for acceptable reasons, are both perfectly clear in their intention to avoid children and wish to make sure that none will result. But it is equally true that it is exclusively in the former case that husband and wife are ready to abstain from intercourse during the fertile period as often as for reasonable motives the birth of another child is not desirable. And when the infertile period recurs, they use their married intimacy to express their mutual love and safeguard their fidelity toward one another. In doing this they certainly give proof of a true and authentic love.

Consequences of Artificial Methods

17. Responsible men can become more deeply convinced of the truth of the doctrine laid down by the Church on this issue if they reflect on the consequences of methods and plans for artificial birth control. Let them first consider how easily this course of action could open wide the way for marital infidelity and a general lowering of moral standards. Not much experience is needed to be fully aware of human weakness and to understand that human beings—and especially the young, who are so exposed to temptation—need incentives to keep the moral law, and it is an evil thing to make it easy for them to break that law. Another effect that gives cause for alarm is that a man who grows accustomed to the use of contraceptive methods may forget the reverence due to a woman, and, disregarding her physical and emotional equilibrium, reduce her to being a mere instrument for the satisfaction of his own desires, no longer considering her as his partner whom he should surround with care and affection.

Finally, careful consideration should be given to the danger of this power passing into the hands of those public authorities who care little for the precepts of the moral law. Who will blame a government which in its attempt to resolve the problems affecting an entire country resorts to the same measures as are regarded as lawful by married people in the solution of a particular family difficulty? Who will prevent public authorities from favoring those contraceptive methods which they consider more effective? Should they regard this as necessary, they may even impose their use on everyone. It could well happen, therefore, that when people, either individually or in family or social life, experience the inherent difficulties of the divine law and are determined to avoid them, they may give into the hands of public authorities the power to intervene in the most personal and intimate responsibility of husband and wife.

Limits to Man's Power

Consequently, unless we are willing that the responsibility of procreating life should be left to the arbitrary decision of men, we must accept that there are certain limits, beyond which it is wrong to go, to the power of man over his own body and its natural functions—limits, let it be said, which no one, whether as a private individual or as a public authority, can lawfully exceed. These limits are expressly imposed because of the reverence due to the whole human organism and its natural functions, in the light of the principles We stated earlier, and in accordance with a correct understanding of the "principle of totality" enunciated by Our predecessor Pope Pius XII. (21)

Concern of the Church

18. It is to be anticipated that perhaps not everyone will easily accept this particular teaching. There is too much clamorous outcry against the voice of the Church, and this is intensified by modern means of communication. But it comes as no surprise to the Church that she, no less than her divine Founder, is destined to be a "sign of contradiction." (22) She does not, because of this, evade the duty imposed on her of proclaiming humbly but firmly the entire moral law, both natural and evangelical.

Since the Church did not make either of these laws, she cannot be their arbiter—only their guardian and interpreter. It could never be right for her to declare lawful what is in fact unlawful, since that, by its very nature, is always opposed to the true good of man.

In preserving intact the whole moral law of marriage, the Church is convinced that she is contributing to the creation of a truly human civilization. She urges man not to betray his personal responsibilities by putting all his faith in technical expedients. In this way she defends the dignity of husband and wife. This course of action shows that the Church, loyal to the example and teaching of the divine Savior, is sincere and unselfish in her regard for men whom she strives to help even now during this earthly pilgrimage "to share God's life as sons of the living God, the Father of all men." (23)

III.
PASTORAL DIRECTIVES

19. Our words would not be an adequate expression of the thought and solicitude of the Church, Mother and Teacher of all peoples, if, after having recalled men to the observance and respect of the divine law regarding matrimony, they did not also support mankind in the honest regulation of birth amid the difficult conditions which today afflict families and peoples. The Church, in fact, cannot act differently toward men than did the Redeemer. She knows their weaknesses, she has compassion on the multitude, she welcomes sinners. But at the same time she cannot do otherwise than teach the law. For it is in fact the law of human life restored to its native truth and guided by the Spirit of God. (24) Observing the Divine Law.

20. The teaching of the Church regarding the proper regulation of birth is a promulgation of the law of God Himself. And yet there is no doubt that to many it will appear not merely difficult but even impossible to observe. Now it is true that like all good things which are outstanding for their nobility and for the benefits which they confer on men, so this law demands from individual men and women, from families and from human society, a resolute purpose and great endurance. Indeed it cannot be observed unless God comes to their help with the grace by which the goodwill of men is sustained and strengthened. But to those who consider this matter diligently it will indeed be evident that this endurance enhances man's dignity and confers benefits on human society.

Value of Self-Discipline

21. The right and lawful ordering of birth demands, first of all, that spouses fully recognize and value the true blessings of family life and that they acquire complete mastery over themselves and their emotions. For if with the aid of reason and of free will they are to control their natural drives, there can be no doubt at all of the need for self-denial. Only then will the expression of love, essential to married life, conform to right order. This is especially clear in the practice of periodic continence. Self-discipline of this kind is a shining witness to the chastity of husband and wife and, far from being a hindrance to their love of one another, transforms it by giving it a more truly human character. And if this self-discipline does demand that they persevere in their purpose and efforts, it has at the same time the salutary effect of enabling husband and wife to develop to their personalities and to be enriched with spiritual blessings. For it brings to family life abundant fruits of tranquility and peace. It helps in solving difficulties of other kinds. It fosters in husband and wife thoughtfulness and loving consideration for one another. It helps them to repel inordinate self-love, which is the opposite of charity. It arouses in them a consciousness of their responsibilities. And finally, it confers upon parents a deeper and more effective influence in the education of their children. As their children grow up, they develop a right sense of values and achieve a serene and harmonious use of their mental and physical powers.

Promotion of Chastity

22. We take this opportunity to address those who are engaged in education and all those whose right and duty it is to provide for the common good of human society. We would call their attention to the need to create an atmosphere favorable to the growth of chastity so that true liberty may prevail over license and the norms of the moral law may be fully safeguarded.

Everything therefore in the modern means of social communication which arouses men's baser passions and encourages low moral standards, as well as every obscenity in the written word and every form of indecency on the stage and screen, should be condemned publicly and unanimously by all those who have at heart the advance of civilization and the safeguarding of the outstanding values of the human spirit. It is quite absurd to defend this kind of depravity in the name of art or culture (25) or by pleading the liberty which may be allowed in this field by the public authorities.

Appeal to Public Authorities

23. And now We wish to speak to rulers of nations. To you most of all is committed the responsibility of safeguarding the common good. You can contribute so much to the preservation of morals. We beg of you, never allow the morals of your peoples to be undermined. The family is the primary unit in the state; do not tolerate any legislation which would introduce into the family those practices which are opposed to the natural law of God. For there are other ways by which a government can and should solve the population problem—that is to say by enacting laws which will assist families and by educating the people wisely so that the moral law and the freedom of the citizens are both safeguarded.

Seeking True Solutions

We are fully aware of the difficulties confronting the public authorities in this matter, especially in the developing countries. In fact, We had in mind the justifiable anxieties which weigh upon them when We published Our encyclical letter *Populorum Progressio*. But now We join Our voice to that of Our predecessor John XXIII of venerable memory, and We make Our own his words: "No statement of the problem and no solution to it is acceptable which does violence to man's essential dignity; those who propose such solutions base them on an utterly materialistic conception of man himself and his life. The only possible solution to this question is one which envisages the social and economic progress both of individuals and of the whole of human society, and which respects and promotes true human values." (26) No one can, without being grossly unfair, make divine Providence responsible for what clearly seems to be the result of misguided governmental policies, of an insufficient sense of social justice, of a selfish accumulation of material goods, and finally of a culpable failure to undertake those initiatives and responsibilities which would raise the standard of living of peoples and their children. (27) If only all governments which were able would do what some are already doing so nobly, and bestir themselves to renew their efforts and their undertakings! There must be no relaxation in the programs of mutual aid between all the branches of the great human family. Here We believe an almost limitless field lies open for the activities of the great international institutions.

To Scientists

24. Our next appeal is to men of science. These can "considerably advance the welfare of marriage and the family and also peace of conscience, if by pooling their efforts they strive to elucidate more thoroughly the conditions favorable to a proper regulation of births." (28) It is supremely desirable, and this was also the mind of Pius XII, that medical science should by the study of natural rhythms succeed in determining a sufficiently secure basis for the chaste limitation of offspring. (29) In this way scientists, especially those who are Catholics, will by their research establish the truth of the Church's claim that "there can be no contradiction between two divine laws—that which governs the transmitting of life and that which governs the fostering of married love." (30)

To Christian Couples

25. And now We turn in a special way to Our own sons and daughters, to those most of all whom God calls to serve Him in the state of marriage. While the Church does indeed hand on to her children the inviolable conditions laid down by God's law, she is also the herald of salvation and through the sacraments she flings wide open the channels of grace through which man is made a new creature responding in charity and true freedom to the design of his Creator and Savior, experiencing too the sweetness of the yoke of Christ. (31)

In humble obedience then to her voice, let Christian husbands and wives be mindful of their vocation to the Christian life, a vocation which, deriving from their Baptism, has been confirmed anew and made more explicit by the Sacrament of Matrimony. For by this sacrament they are strengthened and, one might almost say, consecrated to the faithful fulfillment of their duties. Thus will they realize to the full their calling and bear witness as becomes them, to Christ before the world. (32) For the Lord has entrusted to them the task of making visible to men and women the holiness and joy of the law which united inseparably their love for one another and the cooperation they give to God's love, God who is the Author of human life.

We have no wish at all to pass over in silence the difficulties, at times very great, which beset the lives of Christian married couples. For them, as indeed for every one of us, "the gate is narrow and the way is hard, that leads to life." (33) Nevertheless it is precisely the hope of that life which, like a brightly burning torch, lights up their journey, as, strong in spirit, they strive to live "sober, upright and godly lives in this world," (34) knowing for sure that "the form of this world is passing away." (35)

Recourse to God

For this reason husbands and wives should take up the burden appointed to them, willingly, in the strength of faith and of that hope which "does not disappoint us, because God's love has been poured into our hearts through the Holy Spirit who has been given to us. (36) Then let them implore the help of God with unremitting prayer and, most of all, let them draw grace and charity from that unfailing fount which is the Eucharist. If, however, sin still exercises its hold over them, they are not to lose heart. Rather must they, humble and persevering, have recourse to the mercy of God, abundantly bestowed in the Sacrament of Penance. In this way, for sure, they will be able to reach that perfection of married life which the Apostle sets out in these words: "Husbands, love your wives, as Christ loved the Church.... Even so husbands should love their wives as their own bodies. He who loves his wife loves himself. For no man ever hates his own flesh, but nourishes and cherishes it, as Christ does the Church.... This is a great mystery, and I mean in reference to Christ and the Church; however, let each one of you love his wife as himself, and let the wife fear her husband." (37)

Family Apostolate

26. Among the fruits that ripen if the law of God be resolutely obeyed, the most precious is certainly this, that married couples themselves will often desire to communicate their own experience to others. Thus it comes about that in the fullness of the lay vocation will be included a novel and outstanding form of the apostolate by which, like ministering to like, married couples themselves by the leadership they offer will become apostles to other married couples. And surely among all the forms of the Christian apostolate it is hard to think of one more opportune for the present time. (38)

To Doctors and Nurses

27. Likewise we hold in the highest esteem those doctors and members of the nursing profession who, in the exercise of their calling, endeavor to fulfill the demands of their Christian vocation before any merely human interest. Let them therefore continue constant in their resolution always to support those lines of action which accord with faith and with right reason. And let them strive to win agreement and support for these policies among their professional colleagues. Moreover, they should regard it as an essential part of their skill to make themselves fully proficient in this difficult field of medical knowledge. For then, when married couples ask for their advice, they may be in a position to give them right counsel and to point them in the proper direction. Married couples have a right to expect this much from them.

To Priests

28. And now, beloved sons, you who are priests, you who in virtue of your sacred office act as counselors and spiritual leaders both of individual men and women and of families—We turn to you filled with great confidence. For it is your principal duty—We are speaking especially to you who teach moral theology—to spell out clearly and completely the Church's teaching on marriage. In the performance of your ministry you must be the first to give an example of that sincere obedience, inward as well as outward, which is due to the Magisterium of the Church. For, as you know, the pastors of the Church enjoy a special light of the Holy Spirit in teaching the truth. (39) And this, rather than the arguments they put forward, is why you are bound to such obedience. Nor will it escape you that if men's peace of soul and the unity of the Christian people are to be preserved, then it is of the utmost importance that in moral as well as in dogmatic theology all should obey the Magisterium of the Church and should speak as with one voice. Therefore We make Our own the anxious words of the great Apostle Paul and with all Our heart We renew Our appeal to you: "I appeal to you, brethren, by the name of our Lord Jesus Christ, that all of you agree and that there be no dissensions among you, but that you be united in the same mind and the same judgment." (40)

Christian Compassion

29. Now it is an outstanding manifestation of charity toward souls to omit nothing from the saving doctrine of Christ; but this must always be joined with tolerance and charity, as Christ Himself showed in His conversations and dealings with men. For when He came, not to judge, but to save the world, (41) was He not bitterly severe toward sin, but patient and abounding in mercy toward sinners?

Husbands and wives, therefore, when deeply distressed by reason of the difficulties of their life, must find stamped in the heart and voice of their priest the likeness of the voice and the love of our Redeemer.

So speak with full confidence, beloved sons, convinced that while the Holy Spirit of God is present to the Magisterium proclaiming sound doctrine, He also illumines from within the hearts of the faithful and invites their assent. Teach married couples the necessary way of prayer and prepare them to approach more often with great faith the Sacraments of the Eucharist and of Penance. Let them never lose heart because of their weakness.

To Bishops

30. And now as We come to the end of this encyclical letter, We turn Our mind to you, reverently and lovingly, beloved and venerable brothers in the episcopate, with whom We share more closely the care of the spiritual good of the People of God. For We invite all of you, We implore you, to give a lead to your priests who assist you in the sacred ministry, and to the faithful of your dioceses, and to devote yourselves with all zeal and without delay to safeguarding the holiness of marriage, in order to guide married life to its full human and Christian perfection. Consider this mission as one of your most urgent responsibilities at the present time. As you well know, it calls for concerted pastoral action in every field of human diligence, economic, cultural and social. If simultaneous progress is made in these various fields, then the intimate life of parents and children in the family will be rendered not only more tolerable, but easier and more joyful. And life together in human society will be enriched with fraternal charity and made more stable with true peace when God's design which He conceived for the world is faithfully followed.

A Great Work

31. Venerable brothers, beloved sons, all men of good will, great indeed is the work of education, of progress and of charity to which We now summon all of you. And this We do relying on the unshakable teaching of the Church, which teaching Peter's successor together with his brothers in the Catholic episcopate faithfully guards and interprets. And We are convinced that this truly great work will bring blessings both on the world and on the Church. For man cannot attain that true happiness for which he yearns with all the strength of his spirit, unless he keeps the laws which the Most High God has engraved in his very nature. These laws must be wisely and lovingly observed. On this great work, on all of you and especially on married couples, We implore from the God of all holiness and pity an abundance of heavenly grace as a pledge of which We gladly bestow Our apostolic blessing.

Given at St. Peter's, Rome, on the 25th day of July, the feast of St. James the Apostle, in the year 1968, the sixth of Our pontificate.

PAUL VI

NOTES FOR HUMANAE VITAE

LATIN TEXT: *Acta Apostolicae Sedis*, 60 (1968), 481-503.

ENGLISH TRANSLATION: *The Pope Speaks*, 13 (Fall. 1969), 329-46.

REFERENCES:

(1)   See Pius IX, encyc. letter *Oui pluribus: Pii IX P.M. Acta*, 1, pp. 9-10; St. Pius X encyc. letter *Singulari quadam*: AAS 4 (1912), 658; Pius XI, encyc.letter *Casti connubii*: AAS 22 (1930), 579-581; Pius XII, address *Magnificate Dominum* to the episcopate of the Catholic World: AAS 46 (1954), 671-672; *John* XXIII, encyc. letter *Mater et Magistra*: AAS 53 (1961), 457.

(2)   See *Mt* 28. 18-19.

(3)   See *Mt* 7. 21.

(4)   See Council of Trent Roman Catechism, Part II, ch. 8; Leo XIII, encyc. letter *Arcanum*: *Acta Leonis XIII*, 2 (1880), 26-29; Pius XI, encyc. letter *Divini illius Magistri*: AAS 22 (1930), 58-61; encyc. letter *Casti connubii*: AAS 22 (1930), 545-546; Pius XII, Address to Italian Medico-Biological Union of St. Luke: *Discorsi e radiomessaggi di Pio XII*, VI, 191-192; to Italian Association of Catholic Midwives: AAS 43 (1951), 835-854; to the association known as the Family Campaign, and other family associations: AAS 43 (1951), 857-859; to 7th congress of International Society of Hematology: AAS 50 (1958), 734-735 [TPS VI, 394-395]; John XXIII, encyc. letter *Mater et Magistra*: AAS 53 (1961), 446-447 [TPS VII, 330-331]; Second Vatican Council, *Pastoral Constitution on the Church in the World of Today*, nos. 47-52: AAS 58 (1966), 1067-1074 [TPS XI, 289-295]; Code of Canon Law, canons 1067, 1068 §1, canon 1076, §§1-2.

(5)   See Paul VI, Address to Sacred College of Cardinals: AAS 56 (1964), 588 [TPS IX, 355-356]; to Commission for the Study of Problems of Population, Family and Birth: AAS 57

(1965), 388 [TPS X, 225]; to National Congress of the Italian Society of Obstetrics and Gynecology: AAS 58 (1966), 1168 [TPS XI, 401-403].

(6)   See 1 *Jn* 4. 8.

(7)   *Eph* 3. 15.

(8)   *Pastoral Constitution on the Church in the World of Today*, no. 50: AAS 58 (1966), 1070-1072 [TPS XI, 292-293].

(9)   See St. Thomas, *Summa Theologiae*, I-II, q. 94, art. 2.

(10)   *Pastoral Constitution on the Church in the World of Today*, nos . 50- 5 1: AAS 58 (1 966) 1070-1073 [TPS XI, 292-293].

(11)   See *ibid.*, no. 49: AAS 58 (1966), 1070 [TPS XI, 291-292].

(12)   See Pius XI. encyc. letter *Casti connubi*: AAS 22 (1930), 560; Pius XII, Address to Midwives: AAS 43 (1951), 843.

(13)   See encyc. letter *Mater et Magistra*: AAS 53 (1961), 447 [TPS VII, 331].

(14)   See Council of Trent Roman Catechism, Part II, ch. 8; Pius XI, encyc. letter *Casti connubii*: AAS 22 (1930), 562-564; Pius XII, Address to Medico-Biological Union of St. Luke: *Discorsi e radiomessaggi*, VI, 191-192; Address to Midwives: AAS 43 (1951), 842-843; Address to Family Campaign and other family associations: AAS 43 (1951), 857-859; John XXIII, encyc. letter *Pacem in terris*: AAS 55 (1963), 259-260 [TPS IX, 15-16]; *Pastoral Constitution on the Church in the World of Today*, no. 51: AAS 58 (1966), 1072 [TPS XI, 293].

(15)   See Pius XI, encyc. letter *Casti connubii*: AAS 22 (1930), 565; Decree of the Holy Office, Feb. 22, 1940: AAS 32 (1940), 73; Pius XII, Address to Midwives: AAS 43 (1951), 843-844; to the Society of Hematology: AAS 50 (1958), 734-735 [TPS VI, 394-395].

(16)   See Council of Trent Roman Catechism, Part II, ch. 8; Pius XI, encyc. letter *Casti connubii*: AAS 22 (1930), 559-561; Pius XII, Address to Midwives: AAS 43 (1951), 843; to the Society of Hematology: AAS 50 (1958), 734-735 [TPS VI, 394-395]; John XXIII, encyc. letter *Mater et Magistra*: AAS 53 (1961), 447 [TPS VII, 331].

(17)   See Pius XII, Address to National Congress of Italian Society of the Union of Catholic Jurists: AAS 45 (1953), 798-799 [TPS I, 67-69].

(18)   See *Rom* 3. 8.

(19)   See Pius XII, Address to 26th Congress of Italian Association of Urology: AAS 45 (1953), 674-675; to Society of Hematology: AAS 50 (1958), 734-735 [TPS VI, 394-395].

(20)   See Pius XII, Address to Midwives: AAS 43 (1951), 846.

(21)   See Pius XII, Address to Association of Urology: AAS 45 (1953), 674-675; to leaders and members of Italian Association of Cornea Donors and Italian Association for the Blind: AAS 48 (1956), 461-462 [TPS III, 200-201].

(22)   *Lk* 2. 34.

(23)   See Paul VI, encyc. letter *Populorum progressio*: AAS 59 (1967), 268 [TPS XII, 151].

(24)   See *Rom* 8.

(25)   *Decree on the Media of Social Communication*, nos. 6-7: AAS 56 (1964), 147 [TPS IX, 340-341].

(26)   Encyc. letter *Mater et Magistra*: AAS 53 (1961), 447 [TPS VII, 331].

(27)   See encyc. letter *Populorum progressio*, nos. 48-55: AAS 59 (1967), 281-284 [TPS XII, 160-162].

(28) Second Vatican Council, *Pastoral Constitution on the Church in the World of Today*, no. 52: AAS 58 (1966), 1074 [TPS XI, 294].

(29) Address to Family Campaign and other family associations: AAS 43 (1951), 859.

(30) Second Vatican Council, *Pastoral Constitution on the Church in the World of Today*, no. 51: AAS 58 (1966), 1072 [TPS XI, 293].

(31) See *Mt* 11. 30.

(32) *Pastoral Constitution on the Church in the World of Today*, no. 48: AAS 58 (1966), 1067-1069 [TPS XI,290-291]; *Dogmatic Constitution on the Church*, no. 35: AAS 57 (1965), 40-41 [TPS X, 382-383].

(33) *Mt* 7. 14; see *Heb* 12. 11.

(34) See *Ti* 2. 12.

(35) See 1 *Cor* 7. 31.

(36) *Rom* 5. 5.

(37) *Eph* 5. 25, 28-29, 32-33.

(38) *Dogmatic Constitution on the Church*, nos. 35, 41: AAS 57 (1965), 40-45 [TPS X, 382-383, 386-387; *Pastoral Constitution on the Church in the World of Today*, nos. 48-49: AAS 58 (1966),1067-1070 [TPS XI, 290-292]; *Decree on the Apostolate of the Laity*, no. 11: AAS 58 (1966), 847-849 [TPS XI, 128-129].

(39) *Dogmatic Constitution on the Church*, no. 25: AAS 57 (1965), 29-31 [TPS X, 375-376].

(40) 1 *Cor* 1. 10.

(41) See *Jn* 3. 17.

Bibliography

Amerio, Romano, *Iota Inum,* Italy, Ricciardi Publishing House, 1985.

Brother Michael of the Holy Trinity, *The Third Secret of Fatima,* Rockford Illinois, TAN Books and Publishers, 1992.

Bugnini, Archbishop Annibale, *La Riforma Liturgica,* Italy, 1983.

Carré, Marie, *AA Apostle 1025: Memoirs of an Anti-Apostle,* France, 1972

Casini, Tito, *Nel Fumo di Satana-Verso t'ultimo scontro,* Florence Italy, April 1976.

Clancy, John, *Apostle for our Time: Pope Paul VI,* Avon Books, New York, 1963.

Compton, Piers, *The Broken Cross: Hidden Hand in the Vatican,* Australia, Veritas Publications, 1984.

Davies, Michael, *How the Liturgy Fell Apart: The Enigma of Archbishop Bugnini,* Balwyn Vic Australia, AD Books, 2000; *Liturgical Time Bombs in Vatican II: The Destruction of the Catholic Faith Through Changes in Catholic Worship,* Illinois, TAN Books and Publishers, 2003; *Pope John's Council,* Kansas City, Missouri, Angelus Press, 1977.

Gamber, Fr. Klaus, *The Reform of the Roman Liturgy,* Una Voce Press, 1993.

Graber, Dr. Rudolph (Bishop of Regensburg), *Athanasius and the Church in our Time,* Germany, Van Duren Publishing Company, 1974.

Kolberg, Theodore, *Der Betrug des Jahrhunderts (The Deception of the Century),* Munich, Germany, November 1977; *Umsterz im Vatikan? (An Overthrow in the Vatican?),* Munich, January 1977.

Lefebvre, Archbishop Marcel, *A Bishop Speaks,* Scotland, Una Voce Press, 1963-1974; *I Accuse the Council,* Missouri, Angelus Press, 2nd Edition 1998; *Open Letter to Confused Catholics,* Missouri, Angelus Press, 1986.

Marty, Jean, *Avertissements de l'Au'dela a l'Eglise Contemporaine -- Aveux de l'Enfer,* (Translated from French by Nancy Knowles Smith), France, 1978.

McBride, Ella, *Roses from Heaven,* Orange Texas, Children of Mary, 1988.

Pio, St. Padre, *L'Osservatore Romano,* Rome, October 10, 1968

Rademacher, Mary, *Our Lady of the Roses Mary Help of Mothers (Blue Book),* Lansing Michigan, Apostles of Our Lady, 1981-1983.

Tornielli, Andrea, *Dossie Liturgia Una Babel Programada,* Italy, 1992.

Wiltgen, Fr. Ralph, *The Rhine Flows into the Tiber,* Illinois, TAN Books and Publishers, 1967.

Websites

www.fatima.org

www.smwa.org

www.sspxasia.com

www.vatican.va

All scriptural references taken from the Douay Rheims Catholic Bible, 1899 edition

ABOUT THE AUTHOR

David Martin is the Moderator for St Michael's Radio Program which specializes in the propagation of Catholic prophecy. He has published numerous articles on the Church and has authored two other books, *Vatican II: A Historic Turning Point,* and *Purgatory: The Helpless Cries from Beyond the Veil.*

David gave up a promising career as a concert pianist in 1980 to pursue Catholic evangelism, as expressed in his often repeated phrase: "The mission from Heaven is now my song." He presently resides in Los Angeles, California, where for thirty-two years he has coordinated a Catholic ministry. He is a daily communicant in his parish church and strongly supports Benedict XVI's aspiration to see the Traditional Latin Mass returned to every Catholic parish of the world.